Agatha
Christie

Books by Andrew Norman

HMS Hood: *Pride of the Royal Navy,* The History Press, Stroud, 2009
By Swords Divided: Corfe Castle in the Civil War, Halsgrove, Tiverton, 2003
Tyneham: The Lost Village of Dorset, Halsgrove, Tiverton, 2003
T. E. Lawrence: The Enigma Explained, The History Press, Stroud, 2008
Sir Francis Drake: Behind the Pirate's Mask, Halsgrove, Tiverton, 2004
Dunshay: Reflections on a Dorset Manor House, Halsgrove, Tiverton, 2004
Enid Blyton and her Enchantment with Dorset, Halsgrove, Tiverton, 2005
Thomas Hardy: Christmas Carollings, Halsgrove, Tiverton, 2005
Agatha Christie: The Finished Portrait, Tempus Publishing, Stroud, 2007
Mugabe: Teacher, Revolutionary, Tyrant, The History Press, Stroud, 2008
The Story of George Loveless and the Tolpuddle Martyrs, Halsgrove, Tiverton, 2008
Agatha Christie: The Pitkin Guide, Pitkin Publishing, 2009
Purbeck Personalities, Halsgrove, Tiverton, 2009
Arthur Conan Doyle: The Man behind Sherlock Holmes, The History Press, Stroud, 2009
Father of the Blind: A Portrait of Sir Arthur Pearson, The History Press, Stroud, 2009
Jane Austen: An Unrequited Love, The History Press, Stroud, 2009
Bournemouth's Founders and Famous Visitors, The History Press, Stroud, 2010
Thomas Hardy: Behind the Mask, The History Press, Stroud, 2011
Hitler: Dictator or Puppet, Pen & Sword Books, Barnsley, 2011
Winston Churchill: Portrait of an Unquiet Mind, Pen & Sword Books, Barnsley, 2012
Halsewell: An East Indiaman Reveals her Secrets, Pen & Sword Books, Barnsley, 2013
Charles Darwin: Destroyer of Myths, Pen & Sword Books, Barnsley, 2013
Beatrix Potter: Her Inner World, Pen & Sword Books, Barnsley, 2014
T. E. Lawrence: Tormented Hero, Fonthill Media, Stroud, 2014

Agatha Christie

THE DISAPPEARING NOVELIST

ANDREW NORMAN

FONTHILL

Fonthill Media Limited
www.fonthillmedia.com
office@fonthillmedia.com

First published in the United Kingdom
and the United States of America 2014

ISBN 978-1-78155-262-9

Typeset in 10pt on 13pt Minion Pro

Contents

Agatha Christie Family Tree
(Surviving members)

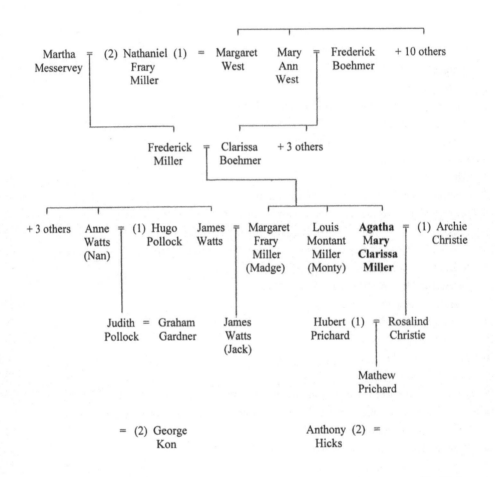

Martha Messervey = (2) Nathaniel Frary Miller (1) = Margaret West

Mary Ann West = Frederick Boehmer + 10 others

Frederick Miller = Clarissa Boehmer + 3 others

+ 3 others

Anne Watts (Nan) = (1) Hugo Pollock

James Watts = Margaret Frary Miller (Madge)

Louis Montant Miller (Monty)

Agatha Mary Clarissa Miller = (1) Archie Christie

Judith Pollock = Graham Gardner

James Watts (Jack)

Hubert Prichard (1) = Rosalind Christie

Mathew Prichard

= (2) George Kon

Anthony (2) = Hicks

= (2) Max Mallowan

Preface

Agatha Christie's mysterious disappearance for eleven days in December 1926 has long been the subject of speculation. When Jared Cade published *Agatha Christie and the Eleven Missing Days* in 1998, in which he implied that it was a premeditated act designed to embarrass her unfaithful husband Archie, to disrupt the weekend which he was spending with his mistress Nancy Neele, and to make him a murder suspect in the eyes of the police,[1] this appeared to be the end of the matter. Cade's assertions were evidently based on information which he had obtained from Judith Gardner, daughter of Agatha's sister Madge's sister-in-law Anne Hadfield Kon (formerly Pollock, née Watts), otherwise known as 'Nan', and Judith's husband Graham in the 1990s; more than seven decades after the event. However, many questions, as yet, remain unanswered.

According to the Gardners, Agatha's disappearance was 'staged',[2] and that if her whereabouts was discovered, she and Nan had agreed that she should 'claim to be suffering from amnesia'.[3] But, if this was the case, then it is pertinent to ask: why did she never admit to perpetrating this alleged hoax? Even when she was 'found out'; why did the three doctors who subsequently examined her (who included an eminent neurologist and a Harley Street psychiatrist) all agree, as did her husband Archie, that her condition was quite genuine? Furthermore, why did she subsequently consult Oxford University's Professor of Moral and Pastoral Theology, in the hope that he would help her to recall this episode of her life of which she had virtually no memory?

Or was there an entirely different explanation? Was Agatha's state of mind, during those lost eleven days, a phenomenon which only a knowledge and understanding of psychiatry can explain? And, during this time, had Agatha become the victim of circumstances completely beyond her control?

CHAPTER 1

A Disappearance

It was Friday, 3 December 1926 and the location, 'Styles', a large, rambling, red brick mansion with mock-Tudor gables and three tall chimneys, situated in Charters Road, Sunningdale, Berkshire. The lady of the house was aged 35, five-feet-seven-inches tall, well built with red hair, grey eyes and a fair complexion. She was dressed in a grey stockinette skirt, green jumper, grey and dark-grey cardigan, and small green velour hat.[1] On the third finger of her left hand she wore a platinum ring with single pearl, but significantly, no wedding ring.[2]

In the early evening, the telephone rang. She picked up the receiver, whereupon the switchboard operator informed her that there was a call for her from London. It was her secretary, Miss Charlotte Fisher, who was also her daughter Rosalind's governess. Scottish, in her early twenties, and well spoken, Miss Fisher had the nickname 'Carlo'. Carlo had been given the day off and had journeyed up to London to meet a friend for dinner, after which the two of them intended to go to a dance together. She enquired as to whether her mistress was all right, and was reassured by the lady of the house that yes, she was quite all right.

Later that evening, just before 10.00 p.m., the lady of the house tiptoed up the stairs and quietly opened the door of her daughter's bedroom. Having made sure that Rosalind, aged seven and her only child, was sleeping soundly, she descended the stairs, pausing in the hallway to say goodbye to the wire-haired terrier, Peter, which had been given to Rosalind as a present following the death of her former pet dog, Joey.[3] She then left by the front door, made her way to the garage, and drove off in her motor car—a grey Morris Cowley.[4]

Meanwhile, having caught the train from London Waterloo to Sunningdale, Carlo arrived back at Styles late that evening. (She would have caught either the 9.40 p.m. from Waterloo, which was scheduled to arrive at Sunningdale at 10.46 p.m., or the 10.40 p.m., arriving at 11.43 p.m).[5] From Sunningdale railway station to Styles was a distance of one and a half miles. As she made her way towards the front door, Carlo paused, noticing that the garage doors had been left wide open, and that the car was not there. As she opened the front door, using her key, Peter the terrier barked to welcome her, and the parlour maid and cook[6] emerged from their beds with worried expressions on their faces. When asked where the mistress of the house was, they told Carlo that she had left unexpectedly two hours earlier, but had not told them where she was going. And where was Rosalind? 'She is upstairs asleep, Miss', was the reply.

Carlo then noticed that her mistress had left a letter for her, instructing her to cancel a hotel reservation which she had previously made for this same weekend at a hotel in Beverley, Yorkshire. 'The letter gave us no idea where she might have gone... it was a personal letter, and only told us that she felt she must leave this house,' Carlo later declared.[7]

According to *The Surrey Advertiser*, at 8 a.m. on Saturday 4 December, a car was found abandoned near Newlands Corner in Surrey by Frederick Dore of Alexander Road, Thames Ditton.[8] (In fact, there were others who laid claim to being the first to discover the abandoned car, including gipsy boy Jack Best.) According to *The Times*, Dore stated that:

> when he found the car the brakes were off and it [i.e. the gear] was in neutral. The running-board and the under-part of the carriage were resting on the bushes. The position of the car suggested to him that it must have been given a push at the top of the hill and sent down deliberately. The lights were off and had evidently been left on until the current became exhausted. If anyone had accidentally run off the road the car would have been pulled up earlier. There was no sign that the brakes had been applied.
>
> A gipsy girl whom he saw going away from the car told him that about midnight she heard a car coming along the track on top of the downs leading from Guildford to the place where the abandoned car was found.[9]

(This latter statement, however, does not fit with the known facts of the case, as will shortly be seen.)

Incidentally, Dore, who was in his early fifties, was an expert on motor cars (being a senior test engineer employed by the A. C. Motor Vehicle Factory at Thames Ditton in Surrey).[10]

Inside the vehicle Dore discovered a fur coat, an attaché case, various articles of clothing, and two pairs of shoes. However, what surprised him most was the discovery of a driving licence, giving details of the vehicle's owner.[11] In the traditional format of the day, this would have been inscribed as follows:

COUNTY OF BERKSHIRE
Licence to drive a MOTOR CAR or MOTOR CYCLE
Agatha Mary Clarissa Christie,
Styles
Sunningdale

To Dore, this must have come as a huge surprise, for Agatha, even though she was at a comparatively early stage in her career, was already one of Britain's leading crime writers, who by this time had seven detective novels to her credit. The first of these, *The Mysterious Affair at Styles*, which was published in 1920, featured the detective character 'Hercule Poirot', who was to become a legend. As for the title of the novel, this derived from the name of her home in Sunningdale—Styles). In the succeeding years, the number of works (novels, plays, and short stories) produced by Agatha were as follows: 1922, one; 1923, thirty; 1924, forty; 1925, seven; 1926, fourteen. They included *The Murder on the Links* (1923) and, in this current year, 1926, *The Murder of Roger Ackroyd*.

According to writer and journalist Laura Thompson (author of *An English Mystery: Agatha Christie*), who was granted 'unique access' to Agatha's 'diaries, letters and family',[12] and who was personally acquainted with Agatha's daughter Rosalind Hicks, it was from the Newlands Corner Hotel that Dore telephoned the police to tell them about his discovery of the car.[13]

It now transpired that prior to this, one Edward McAlister, of Merrow near Guildford, had encountered a woman and her car in that same vicinity. Subsequently, he said that he was 'convinced that the woman was Mrs Christie'.[14]

According to *The Times*, McAlister told the police that on the morning of Saturday 4 December:

> about 400 yards from the top of Newlands Corner on the road leading over Merrow Downs he saw a grey car. A lady came out from behind the car and asked if he would start it. The radiator was quite cold. The woman had no coat or hat on, and was wearing a grey jumper. After some time he got the car started and the woman drove the car very slowly away downhill [i.e. down Trodd's Lane] towards Merrow [a village 1½ miles to the north-west], and away from Newlands Corner. If that was the car that was abandoned the woman must have turned round and driven up the hill behind him. He could see nobody else about.[15]

It therefore appears, that in the dark, Agatha had turned right off the A25 a short distance before she should have done, and had found herself in Trodd's Lane, rather than in Water Lane, as she had intended.

A subsequent report in the *Surrey Advertiser* sheds further light on the matter:

> At 6.20 a.m. on Saturday morning a man started up a car for a woman, who he thinks was Mrs Christie, along the road leading from Newlands Corner to Merrow [i.e. Trodd's Lane].

The man in question was 'Edward McAlister of Holt Hurst, Trodds Lane, Merrow, who works at the gravel pits'. (This was, in fact, a reference to chalk pits, rather than gravel pits.) By coincidence, it was above one of these very pits that Agatha's motor car was subsequently discovered.[16]

McAlister himself stated as follows:

> About 6.20 on Saturday morning I was going to work up Merrow Lane [which skirted the east side of Guildford], and about 300 yards below the signpost at the junction of the roads at Newlands Corner [i.e. the junction of Trodds Lane and the A25], I saw a motor car with a woman standing at the back of the car. The front of the car was [pointing] towards Merrow, as if it had been proceeding in that direction. She said to me: 'Would you mind starting up my car for me, please?'. I said: 'I will have a try.' I got off my bicycle and started up the car, after some little trouble. The radiator was cold. The lights of the car were on.

(As regards 'lighting-up times', the regulations stated that front and rear lights must be switched on from half an hour after sunset until half an hour before sunrise at all times, apart from during the official 'Summer Time'.[17]   On that day sunrise would have occurred at 7.48 a.m., with twilight commencing at about 7.10 a.m.[18]

> She was, he told our representative, wearing a grey worsted jumper, and a grey skirt, but had no hat. Her hair was bobbed. When he started up the car she said: 'That's splendid. Thanks very much.' Then she got into the car and drove very slowly down the hill towards Merrow.
>
> Mr. McAlister did not see the woman very clearly because it was dark at the time. She did not seem distraught, nor particularly distressed, but seemed a little strange, which he put down to the worry with the car.[19]

According to *The Times*, McAlister told the police that 'the woman's hair—she was hatless—was covered with hoar frost'.[20] (Whereas it is possible that the frost had settled on Agatha's hair, what is more likely is that it came from the branch of a bush which she inadvertently brushed against.)

> At about five minutes to eight a gipsy boy named [Jack] Best, saw the car in the bush, which is about 30 yards from the main road, and a little below the brow of the hill on the Albury side. He looked at it and passed on.[21]

It was not until 11.00 a.m. that Saturday morning that Superintendent William Kenward, Deputy Chief Constable of Surrey, stated that he first learnt of the discovery of the abandoned car.[22] Kenward was based at the County Police Headquarters, Woodbridge Road, Guildford,[23] that city being located about three miles from Newlands Corner. Such a time delay is not easy to explain, given that Frederick Dore discovered the car at 8 a.m. and telephoned the police from the nearby Newlands Corner Hotel, which is only about 1½ miles from the chalk pit.

On hearing the news, Kenward duly contacted his colleagues in the Surrey Constabulary, in whose jurisdiction Agatha's home Styles, Sunningdale, lay. The outcome was that, under the direction of Superintendent Charles Goddard of Berkshire Constabulary's Wokingham Division, a policeman was dispatched to Styles to see if any further light could be shed on the matter.[24]

At Styles the policeman was told by Carlo that yes, Agatha had left the house the previous evening in her motor car, and that she had not yet returned. Carlo herself had not been present at the time, but had learned as much from the household staff. As for Agatha's husband Archie, for that weekend, he had:

> accepted an invitation to join a house party given by Mr. and Mrs. S. James [i.e. Mr Sam James and his wife Madge] at Hurstmore Cottage, Godalming, [Surrey] where Miss Neele had also been invited. There were just the four of them and no other guests.[25]

This was a reference to Archie's mistress Nancy Neele, a secretary in the city who lived with her parents at Croxley Green, Rickmansworth, Hertfordshire, and whom Archie had first met in early 1925.[26]

Carlo had last seen her mistress the previous morning. As to her mistress's state of mind, Agatha had:

> been in ill health for a very considerable time. She felt very keenly the loss of her mother. It preyed upon her so because they had never been separated until Mrs Miller had died.[27]

(Agatha's mother Mrs Clara Miller had died that spring, on 5 April.)

As for Carlo herself, on the evening of Thursday 2 December, after dinner, she had accompanied Mrs Christie to Ascot, where they had attended their weekly dancing class together.[28] (Agatha 'had recently taken up dancing lessons to learn some of the new steps as a therapeutic hobby to try to dispel her constant depression'.[29]) On Friday, Carlo had spent her day off in London. She had caught the train home, arriving at Styles late that evening, by which time Mrs Christie had already departed.

However, Mrs Christie had left a letter for Carlo. This was seen years later by Janet Morgan (author of *Agatha Christie: A Biography*, who was acquainted with Agatha's daughter Rosalind, and who had been granted privileged access to the Christie family archives). Agatha was 'exceedingly distraught', and she informed Carlo that 'in the circumstances', she:

did not believe she could go to Yorkshire [for the weekend, as she had previously planned], that she was going away and would let Carlo know where she was. Its underlying theme was that Agatha had been treated unjustly; the letter ended 'It just isn't fair'. It was not, it seems, the sort of letter that would be left behind by someone intending to kill herself, but rather, something written by a person who felt that, though she had been badly treated, she was still in control of her own fate, as long as—and this Agatha stressed in the letter—she could 'get away from here'.[30]

Continued Janet, 'This was the letter Carlo gave to the police. It was returned after Agatha was found.'[31] Rosalind showed me the letter on one of my early visits to Greenway'.[32]

The policeman proceeded to acquaint Carlo of the news that Agatha's abandoned motor car had been discovered at Newlands Corner; intelligence that would have set alarm bells ringing in Carlo's mind. 'I don't think anything has given me more pleasure... than my dear bottle-nosed Morris Cowley',[33] Agatha had once declared, and it was therefore hard to imagine that she would have abandoned the vehicle of her own free will. The policeman reassured Carlo that everything possible was being done to locate her mistress, and that a search of the area around Newlands Corner was already under way. He then proceeded to interview the domestic staff.

They informed him that the previous morning, Friday, Mrs Christie had gone out in her motor car. She had not said where she was going, but she returned home in time for luncheon. In the afternoon she ventured out once again, taking her daughter Rosalind with her to visit her mother-in-law Mrs Helmsley, who lived at 'Middle Lodge', Deepdene, Dorking—20 miles away. The staff confirmed that Agatha returned home in time for dinner.[34]

When did Carlo last see Colonel Christie, the policeman enquired? 'Yesterday morning,' she replied. He left home at 9.15 a.m., for work in the City, prior to spending the weekend with friends, at Godalming.

On the policeman's instructions, Carlo then telephoned Colonel Christie to tell him that a police car would be dispatched to Godalming to collect him and bring him back to Styles. Archie duly arrived home, but before the policeman had a chance to question him, he was intercepted by Carlo, who handed him a letter, left for him by Agatha. He opened it and read it, but failed to mention this fact to the police.[35] According to Laura Thompson, Archie burned this letter 'before anyone else could read it'.[36]

As for the letter that Agatha had left for Carlo 'asking her to cancel the booking at the hotel in Beverley', this 'Carlo gave [to] the police [and it] was returned after Agatha was found'.[37]

Carlo now sent to London to her sister Mary Fisher, asking her to come down to Styles to keep her company. This, Mary did and she stayed for the duration of Agatha's disappearance.[38] Meanwhile, Agatha's car:

was taken to the Guildford Garage, Epsom Road, on Saturday afternoon [4 December], and to Sunningdale the next day [i.e. it was returned to Styles]. An employee of the garage who fetched it said that, when he saw the car, which was a four-seater Morris-Cowley, the brakes were off but it was in gear. The bonnet was slightly damaged, the speedometer cable broken, and the wing a little bent. The electric battery was run down [i.e. flat].[39]

* * *

What had prompted Agatha to leave home without forewarning anybody? Why had she chosen to leave at 10 p.m., knowing that Rosalind's governess Carlo, would not return until about midnight? What was she doing in remote downland near Newlands Corner in Surrey, fourteen miles away from her home at Sunningdale in Berkshire, on a cold night and in the middle of winter? And why, given the adverse weather conditions, was she not wearing her fur coat, which had been left behind in the vehicle?

Had Agatha simply abandoned the car at the top of the slope and let it run down the track and into the bushes, as Frederick Dore believed, or had it been her intention to drive the car into the quarry (chalk pit) with herself inside it, in a suicide attempt? Here was a mystery worthy of the great detective writer herself; one which captured the imagination of the public, and of which the newspapers took full advantage, taking notice of each and every new development and splashing photographs of the car, the crash scene, the police, the searches, and of course, Agatha and her family all over their front pages. As might be imagined, the disappearance of arguably the most famous female crime writer in England was, for the press, nothing short of manna from heaven!

CHAPTER 2

Superintendent Kenward and
the Search for Agatha

William Kenward was born at King's Lynn in Norfolk in 1876. Heavily built, with moustache and the inevitable trilby hat, he was now aged fifty. An experienced officer, he had joined the Surrey Constabulary in 1899 at the age of twenty-three. Over the course of the next twenty years he had risen through the ranks, from Constable, Third Class, to Inspector.

Kenward was a gifted, brave, and diligent officer, who received many police commendations for his 'excellent detective work, ability, energy', and 'courage'. In addition, on a personal level, he was a man who cared deeply, both for humans and for animals, as Tom Roberts, a young police constable assigned to the Christie case, testified.[1]

As I got to know Mr Kenward better I found him to be a man of great compassion; he would show this in many ways while doing his utmost to avoid publicity.[2]

He held the rank of Superintendent and Deputy Chief Constable [at Guildford] from 1922 until 1931.

It would, therefore, have been profoundly upsetting to the Superintendent to think that Agatha might be lying somewhere in the wilds of the countryside near Newlands Corner; perhaps having been injured, or even worse.

According to *The Times* newspaper, on Monday 6 December:

there were altogether about 100 police and others engaged in the search in the neighbourhood near where the abandoned car was found, and they had a very difficult task. The Downs [an area of high ground, stretching from Newlands Corner westward, almost as far as Guildford, and eastward for six miles in the direction of Dorking] are densely wooded in parts, with undergrowth very hard to penetrate. Several ponds were dragged, including the Silent Pool at the foot of Newlands Corner on the Dorking side, the water of which is deep but crystal clear. Albury Mill Pond, a short distance away, was also dragged, but owing to the weed it was impossible to make a thorough search. The searchers… covered a good deal of country on both sides of the Downs, and searched the water courses in the valley, almost into Guildford, but without result. They continued their work until darkness set in…[3]

That same day, Archie visited Scotland Yard and appealed to that organisation to intervene, but was told that this was not possible without a request for assistance from either the Surrey or the Berkshire Police.[4] This request was not forthcoming.

On the afternoon of Tuesday 7 December 'two civilian aeroplanes took part in the search', but again to no avail.

They crossed and re-crossed the wooded downs and circled many times around the spot where the car was found abandoned, but it is understood that they discovered nothing that would assist in solving the mystery.[5]

According to the *Surrey Advertiser*

Particularly large parties participated in the search on Tuesday and Thursday and, armed with long sticks, examined closely the bushes and bracken, peered into hollows, and tramped through woods and undergrowth. On Thursday, a farm tractor was used to open tracks through the clumps of bushes and tangled undergrowth. During the afternoon it broke down.[6]

Inquiries have also been made of gipsies in the district, including those at Hurtwood, but without success, and reports from persons in London, Petersham, Woolwich, Godalming, Milford, and Little London (near Albury) of their having seen a woman resembling Mrs Christie have been investigated, but have led nowhere.[7]

The *Daily News* now offered a reward of £100 'for anyone furnishing information which would lead to Mrs Christie's recovery'.[8]

On Wednesday 8 December, *The Times* newspaper reported that late the previous evening it had received information that Colonel Christie's brother Captain Campbell Christie of The Royal Military Academy, Woolwich (who had been decorated for bravery in the First World War), had also received a letter from Agatha, addressed from Styles and therefore composed by her before she left home on the Friday evening, which he had discovered when he went into his office the previous Sunday. According to *The Times*, the letter had informed Campbell that Agatha was 'in ill health and was going to a Yorkshire spa'.[9] A spa, in this context, is a commercial establishment offering health and beauty treatment through such means as steam baths, exercise equipment, and massage. The spa may be situated at a place where a natural spring wells up out of the ground, which contains minerals considered to have health-giving properties. It should be noted that there were several spa resorts in Yorkshire, including Scarborough, Askern, Boston Spa, Ilkley, Knaresborough, and the most famous one of all, Harrogate.

Having subsequently learnt of his sister-in-law's disappearance, Campbell looked for the letter but found he had mislaid it. However, he did manage to retrieve the envelope in which the letter had been posted, and this he immediately forwarded to his brother Archie.[10]

On Thursday 9 December, *The Times reported that:*

The postmark on the letter was well defined and enquiries were made yesterday in the 'SW1' [South West 1] postal district [of London] in the hope of discovering the sender of the letter.[11]

According to Janet Morgan, the postmark also indicated the time and date, '9.45 [a.m., Saturday] December 4',[12] indicating that it had been posted in the 'South-West' district of London within an hour or two of this time. (The main London post offices opened for the day at 6.45 a.m. and most other London post offices at 7.30 a.m.)[13] The question was, had Agatha posted this letter herself and, if so, how had she managed to travel from Newlands Corner to London, and what was she doing in the capital city at that time of the morning?

It may be assumed that Agatha wrote to Campbell under her real name, which is significant, as will be seen, and that her letter did not ring any alarm bells in her brother-in-law's mind, otherwise he would surely have acted upon it immediately.

The Times declared that the Surrey Constabulary, on the basis of the above information provided by Campbell and passed on to them by his brother Archie, 'have communicated with certain centres in Yorkshire, and as a result are satisfied, it is understood, that Mrs Christie is not in that county'.[14] The investigators had drawn a blank.

Meanwhile, on the previous day, Wednesday 8 December, according to *The Times*

> The Guildford and Shere Beagles Hunt met in the neighbourhood of Newlands Corner... the fixture having been arranged some time ago, and at the request of the police they kept a special look-out. Fifteen couples of hounds and many huntsmen and followers on foot attended the meet.

The newspaper also reported that another 'big and intensive search of the countryside' was planned, commencing at 10.00 a.m. the following morning, to 'thoroughly scour the ground over a radius of five miles. It is probable that a request will be made for the full aid of Scotland Yard'.[15]

Meanwhile, with Styles being besieged by the gentlemen of the Press, a policeman stood guard at the front and another at the rear, and Rosalind found herself being taken to school in a police car!

As the week progressed, the search for Agatha was unrelenting. On Thursday 9 December, the searchers were:

> organized in two main parties... under the direction of Supt Kenward, Deputy Chief Constable of Surrey; Supt Bosher of Woking; and Supt Porl of Godalming. One [group] worked from the direction of Dorking towards Newlands Corner... and the other from Guildford. They met at Newlands Corner at dusk..., a weary body of men, after searching the Downs, woods and gorseland for seven hours. Meanwhile, a small party searched in and around Newlands Corner. [However] The whole search has proved fruitless [and] not the slightest clue has been found.[16]

According to Gwen Robyns, journalist and author of *The Mystery of Agatha Christie:*[17]

> On Thursday morning [9 December] when there was still no news, Colonel Christie went to his office in London. During the week police had been on guard at his house and monitored his telephone calls.
>
> When he called at his office on the sixth floor of the Rio Tinto Company in the City of London, he rode up in the elevator with Mr Sebastian Earl, who had the office next door to him.... [According to Earl] He was in a terribly nervous state and said that the police had followed him up Broad Street and all the way to the office and were now waiting outside. 'They think I've murdered my wife,' he said.[18]

According to *The Scotsman* newspaper, 'four or five miles to the south of Newlands Corner is one of the largest permanent gipsy encampments in that part of the country', and on that same day, 'it was visited by a force of about fifty police[men] who questioned many of the camp dwellers',[19] But again it was to no avail.

For three hours during the afternoon of Thursday 9 December, Archie himself, together with:

his wife's favourite wire-haired terrier Peter [who, as already mentioned, belonged, in fact, to Rosalind], and accompanied by Supt Kenward, searched every bush near the spot where the abandoned car was found. But the whimpering dog could find no trace of its mistress.[20]

Said Archie:

Peter, our little dog… made straight down the hill from the place where the car was found. He did that of his own accord and then stopped. He circled round a few chalk pits and so on, but found nothing.[21]

An aeroplane again took part in the search and a caterpillar tractor… tore up bushes and thick hedges, whilst scores of dogs, some belonging to the police and others to members of the public, investigated the swampy ground, all with a negative result.[22]

Meanwhile, the Colonel declared that his telephone was constantly ringing; all manner of people were asking about his wife, and even clairvoyants had offered to help him find her!

Superintendent Kenward tried to keep the costs of the search for Agatha to a minimum. For example, by diverting regular police 'from quiet country districts where their services were not likely to be especially needed'.[23] When later asked about this by the Home Office, he is quoted as saying:

Cost. Could not give a definite figure but said extra expenditure consequent on Christie case was about £25—travelling and subsistence. It might be a few shgs [shillings] more but nothing substantial.[24]

This was 'made up chiefly for hire of conveyances, and refreshments for the special constables'.[25]

Special steps. All talk of divers, aeroplanes and other stunts was merely press invention. Police certainly took no such steps and he is certain nobody else did.[26]

Nevertheless, despite Kenward's assertions to the contrary, it is certain that 'civilian aeroplanes' *did*, in fact, participate in the search.

Diversion from other duties. Police only concerned themselves with the actual search for two days—about thirty on one day and thirty-eight [on] another—and this was the total cost of the diversion from other duties. As a matter of fact, a very large number of police who had interested themselves in the case searched in their own time, quite unofficially, particularly on the Sunday.[27]

It is a fact that about a dozen of the three dozen [regular police officers] employed voluntarily came and helped on their weekly rest day.[28]

Furthermore, said Kenward, when Archie was 'approached in regard to the expenses [he] declined to pay the amount mentioned, saying that he is of the opinion it is entirely a police matter'.[29] Finally, the Superintendent declared:

No members of the Metropolitan Police were specially detailed for this purpose, and no cost was incurred by the Metropolitan Police. A description of the missing person was published in Informations, in the usual way.[30]

CHAPTER 3

Archie's Account

Agatha's husband Archie Christie, aged 37, was a former Royal Air Force Officer, and had, like his brother Campbell, been decorated for bravery during the First World War. He spoke frankly about the situation.

It is quite true that my wife had discussed the possibility of disappearing at will. Some time ago she told her sister [Madge], 'I could disappear if I wished and set about it carefully'. They were discussing something that appeared in the papers I think. That shows that the possibility of engineering a disappearance had been running through her mind, probably for the purpose of her work. Personally, I feel that is what happened. At any rate, I am buoying myself up with that belief.[1]

Archie opined that there were 'three possible explanations' for his wife's disappearance:

Voluntarily
Loss of memory
Suicide

I am inclined to the first, although, of course, it may be loss of memory as a result of her highly nervous state.

I do not believe this is a case of suicide. She never threatened suicide, but if she did contemplate that, I am sure her mind would turn to poison. I do not mean that she has ever discussed the question of taking poison, but that she used poison very largely in her stories.[2]

(N.B. Up until the year 1961, suicide, in the United Kingdom, was a criminal offence.) In this context, one of the 'stories' which Archie may have had in mind was Agatha's novel *The Cornish Mystery*, published in 1923 in which Mrs Pengelly appeals to Hercule Poirot for help, in the belief that her husband was trying to poison her! Continued Archie:

I have remonstrated with her in regard to this form of death. But her mind always turned to it. If she wanted to get poison, I am sure she could have done so. She was very clever at getting anything she wanted.

But against the theory of suicide you have to remember this: if a person intends to end his life he does not take the trouble to go miles away and then remove a heavy coat and walk off into the blue before doing it. That is one reason why I do not think my wife has taken her life.[3]

As for the couple's movements over the previous few days, Archie stated as follows. On Wednesday, Agatha:

> went to town [London] where she had a dinner engagement, and stayed the night at the Forum Club. I also had a dinner engagement in town with my old RAF squadron, so I too did not return home that night.[4]
>
> I do not know what my wife did on Thursday morning, but I know that in the afternoon she went to see her agents.[5] [Literary agents Hughes Massie Limited.[6]] She told me that they had been talking about her new [i.e. forthcoming] novel *The Mystery of the Blue Train*, which she could not complete. I gathered that they rather pressed her for it and also wanted to know something about two stories she had to write to complete a series of six for America.
>
> I think she was also rather worried about turning another series of hers—*The Big Four*—into book form. It did not, however, appear to affect her, for after dinner on Thursday evening she went off with her secretary Miss Fisher, to a dancing class or something at Ascot.[7]

Finally, said Archie, on the morning of Agatha's disappearance:

> I left home at 9.15 a.m. in the ordinary way, and that was the last time I saw my wife. I knew that she had arranged to go to Yorkshire for the weekend. I understand that in the morning she went motoring and then lunched alone. In the afternoon she went to see my mother [Mrs Helmsley] at Dorking. She returned here in time for dinner, which she took alone.[8]

Precisely where Agatha drove to that Friday morning, therefore remains a mystery.

> I do not know what happened after that: I only know what I have been told by the servants. I imagine, however, that she got into such a state that she could not sit down quietly to read or work. I have got into that state myself many a time and have gone out for a walk just aimlessly. That, I think, is what my wife did, but instead of walking she took the car, a four-seater, and drove off.[9]
>
> She apparently packed a small suitcase before she went and took it with her. It was found in the car with all its contents complete, so far as we know. Her fur coat was there too. She must have taken it off when she abandoned the car and walked off.
>
> The servants did not notice anything particularly strange about her, and when Miss Fisher, who had gone to London, rang up in the evening to see if she was wanted, my wife was all right.

He then mentioned the letter ['note'], which Agatha had left for Carlo, asking 'for the arrangements for the Yorkshire visit that weekend to be cancelled...', and telling her secretary that she 'was going for a run round' in her motor car, and 'would let her know on the morrow where she was'. And he ended by saying:

> That is all I know, and I need hardly tell you that the suspense of the uncertainty is terrible.[10]

When the *Daily Mail* reporter 'directed Col. Christie's attention to certain rumours which have gained currency in Sunningdale and elsewhere', Archie replied indignantly and defensively:

It is absolutely untrue to suggest there was anything in the nature of a row or tiff between my wife and myself on Friday morning. She was perfectly well—that is to say as well as she had been for months past. She knew I was going away for the weekend: she knew who were going to be the members of the little party at the house at which I was going to stay, and neither then nor at any time did she raise the slightest objection. My wife has never made the slightest objection to any of my friends, all of whom she knew.

I strongly deprecate introducing any tittle-tattle into this matter. That will not help me to find my wife—that is what I want to do.

However, said the *Daily Mail's* reporter:

Friends of Mrs Christie have told me today that recently she has been particularly depressed, and that on one occasion she said, 'If I do not leave Sunningdale, Sunningdale will be the end of me.'[11]

* * *

On Friday 10 December, which was almost a week after Agatha's disappearance, Superintendent Kenward travelled to Wokingham to consult with Superintendent Goddard of the Berkshire Constabulary. He then proposed to travel on to London, presumably for a consultation with Scotland Yard.[12]

On Saturday 11 December, the *Surrey Advertiser* reported that:

Plantations above and below Newlands Corner have been combed as effectively as the forces available would permit; clues have been followed up and theories examined, but the question remains—where is Mrs Christie?[13]

According to Laura Thompson, *The Sketch:*

informed its readers that 'Colonel Christie was today [11 December] invited to call upon Deputy Chief Constable Kenward' in order to discuss the letter [from Agatha] that he had destroyed.[14]

'I have handled many important cases during my career', declared a weary Superintendent Kenward, 'but this is the most baffling mystery ever set me for solution.'[15]

Tom Roberts had joined the Surrey Constabulary that very year, 1926, at the age of twenty. He described Superintendent Kenward as 'a huge man with penetrating eyes', who, at his interview, 'asked me why I wanted to become a policeman'.[16] Following Agatha's disappearance, Roberts 'was called upon to search the area at Newlands Corner for clues'.[17] He observed that 'the bushes were crushed and broken from the impact of the car, but they had prevented it from falling into the chalk pit'.[18] Roberts subsequently expressed the following opinion.

Looking back, it seems that Mrs Christie had chosen this site deliberately, as she could leave her car there and then walk to the Guildford-Waterloo main-line station at West Clandon, and disappear.[19]

Laura Thompson stated, however, that it was not to Clandon Station (two and a quarter miles to the north of the chalk pit) that Agatha made her way, but to Chilworth Station (one and three quarter miles south west of the chalk pit), from where she caught a train to Waterloo. However, this is unlikely, because although Chilworth Station was marginally nearer, it was not on the main line to Waterloo, so Agatha would have had to change trains at Guildford in order to complete her journey.

Janet Morgan, on the other hand, stated that Agatha caught the train from Guildford,[20] which is possible, but unlikely—Guildford Station being considerably further from the chalk pit than Clandon, i.e. about three and a half miles.

* * *

Archie's impression, when he left home on the Friday morning, was that Agatha's plan was to go to Yorkshire for the weekend. However, he subsequently learnt from the letter which Agatha had left for Carlo that Agatha had instructed that the booking for the hotel in Beverley, Yorkshire be cancelled. Therefore, he evidently had no more idea of where Agatha had gone than had Carlo.

CHAPTER 4

Superintendent Goddard Begs to Differ

Charles Goddard, born in 1861 at Eaton Hastings, Berkshire, had joined the Berkshire Constabulary in 1881 at the age of twenty. He was, therefore, fifteen years senior to Superintendent Kenward of the Surrey Constabulary. Described as 'a comparatively short man' and a 'colourful figure', he, like Kenward, had risen through the ranks. In 1924, Goddard was awarded the King's Police Medal for Meritorious Service.[1]

In regard to Agatha's disappearance, Goddard took a different view from that of his colleague Superintendent Kenward. 'I do not accept the theory that Mrs Christie committed suicide at Newlands Corner,' he declared.

There is no evidence that I can find to support that theory, nor do I see any special reason to assume that she is dead.[2] When Mrs Christie has worked out her problem she will return.[3]

Goddard therefore focused his search on other parts of the country,[4] including the West of England, Yorkshire, Lancashire, and North Wales.

Frankly, I had nothing to go on save my own deductions on the facts before me. But I may admit this. I knew that when she left her house it was her intention to drive around for a little while until she had made up her mind what she was going to do. An important factor, to my mind, was the finding of the fur coat in the abandoned car. A woman who was going to commit suicide, I argued, would not get out of a car, take off her coat, and walk a considerable distance away. [This, as already mentioned, was also Archie's view.] She would in all probability, having made up her mind, taken her life where she sat.

Another factor in my deduction was the manner in which Mrs Christie was dressed. She could have passed the night comfortably driving around in her car wearing a fur coat, and then when she had made up her mind to leave the car had discarded the coat, which was too heavy for walking in. Under the fur coat she wore warm clothing of the sort a woman wears for country walks.

I thought from all these factors she had walked from her car and had taken a train for some very definite destination. Hence I got busy with posters, circulating them to all police stations.[5]

The posters to which Goddard referred stated as follows:

BERKSHIRE CONSTABULARY, WOKINGHAM DIVISION. 9 December 1926.
MISSING from her home The Styles Sunningdale in this Division.
Mrs Agatha Mary Clarissa CHRISTIE

(WIFE OF COLONEL A. CHRISTIE)

AGE 35 YEARS, HEIGHT 5 ft 7 in, HAIR RED (Shingled), NATURAL TEETH, EYES GREY, COMPLEXION FAIR, WELL BUILT.

There followed details of the circumstances of Agatha's disappearance, her apparel, and her motor vehicle, together with an image of Agatha in a slightly stooped posture and holding her handbag. Finally, the posters read:

> Should this lady be seen or any information regarding her be obtained please communicate to any Police Station, or to CHARLES GODDARD, Superintendent, WOKINGHAM. Telephone No. 11 Wokingham.

Superintendent Kenward, however, persisted in his belief that 'Mrs Christie is dead, and that her body is somewhere near Newlands Corner',[6] and this, despite the fact that Agatha had evidently posted a letter to Campbell Christie from London early that Saturday morning.

On Sunday 12 December, nine days after Agatha's disappearance, the search of the countryside around Newlands Corner reached its apotheosis. Despite the presence of:

> a very heavy mist, there was a large gathering of people.... Among the early arrivals was a breeder and exhibitor of bloodhounds, who brought with her three dogs, which, at the suggestion of Deputy Chief Constable Kenward, were first taken along the old chalk road which runs towards Dorking, and afterwards explored a tract of country near the Silent Pool.
>
> At times the roads were blocked with traffic, and parked cars covered the whole of the plateau where the abandoned motor-car was found. Altogether over 400 cars and many motor-cycles arrived during the day.[7]

However, according to *The Times*, although this endeavour had once again proved fruitless, Kenward was not finished yet, for he now proposed to search an area of forty square miles, extending 'along the Downs from the neighbourhood of Newlands Corner to Ranmore Common near Dorking, and embracing Albury and Hurtwood'. The entire area was to be mapped out and divided into sections, and a note made of all its pools and ravines. Kenward estimated that this sectional 'comb-out' would take about a week. In addition, he had received an offer from a London firm, of a diver and equipment to search the pools, and he stated that he would probably avail himself of this offer.[8] (It appears, however, that this was not the case, for Kenward subsequently stated that no divers were employed by the police.)

> With regard to the question of volunteer searchers, Mr. Kenward said, it would probably be as well for the police to have the ground to themselves for a day or two, but about eighty members of the Aldershot Motor Cycling Club had offered their services for Tuesday (14 December).[9]

* * *

The question to be asked was, who would be proved right about Agatha—Kenward or Goddard?

CHAPTER 5

Meanwhile, at Harrogate...

According to Mr W. Taylor, the Manager of the Hydropathic Hotel (known as 'The Hydro'), Harrogate, in Yorkshire, a lady arrived there on Saturday 4 December in a taxi cab. 'She asked for a bedroom *en pension* terms [i.e. at a fixed rate for board and lodging], which indicated that her stay there was to be a prolonged one, and was given a good room on the first floor, fitted with hot and cold water.[1]

I did not see her myself, but I believe that the price quoted to her was seven guineas a week. She accepted this without hesitation. Indeed, all the time she was here she seemed to have as much money as she wanted.[2]

The *Harrogate Advertiser*, referring to the same lady, stated that she:

arrived at the Hydro late in the afternoon of Saturday 4 December, and registered under the name of Mrs Teresa Neele of Cape Town, South Africa. She had little luggage with her.

However, in the same article it was stated that the lady had arrived at The Hydro 'on Saturday night, December 4'.[3]

Continued Mr Taylor, 'For the first three days of her stay I did not particularly notice her. We had many guests and I am a busy man....' He did, however, confirm that:

From the first, her life in the Hydro was exactly similar to that of our other guests. She took her meals in the public dining-room, only occasionally having her breakfast in bed. She talked willingly enough with her fellow-guests and during the day sometimes went for walks with them. In the evening we sometimes have singing and dancing in the lounge.

In these activities Mrs Neele:

took an enthusiastic part. She sang several songs—what they were I do not remember, for I am not musical—and she danced often, mixing freely with the young people staying at the Hydro.[4]

But, said Taylor:

when she had been here about four days my wife said to me: 'I believe that lady is Mrs Christie!' My answer was: 'Don't be so absurd!'[5]

According to the *Daily Mail's* special correspondent:

> She arrived on December 4 without, I understand, any luggage. The first night, however, she wore evening dress at dinner and, it is understood, she has bought a good many clothes since she has been here. She has worn evening clothes every night at dinner with a fancy scarf round her shoulders.[6]

This statement is somewhat puzzling, as Mrs Neele had evidently not brought a suitcase with her, and by the time of her arrival late on Saturday, and for the whole of Sunday, the shops would have been closed. Gwen Robyns, on the other hand, stated that when Agatha attended the dance on the evening of Saturday 4 December, 'she was wearing the short, knitted dress that she disappeared in...', rather than evening dress. Furthermore, Robyns went on to say that, according to Miss Corbett, pianist at The Hydro, 'On Monday she [Mrs Neele] apparently went shopping because from then on she appeared in different clothes every day.'[7] This explanation by Robyns therefore seems to be altogether more plausible.

Continued the *Daily Mail*:

> For the first few days she spoke to scarcely anybody, but since then she has made a number of friends. On two occasions she has played billiards, but her playing is indifferent, and she has rarely made [i.e. scored] more than five or six at a time.
>
> On several occasions she has sung for the visitors in the drawing-room. She plays the piano and sings charmingly. Last Sunday night [12 December, nine days after her arrival] she took part in a house concert in the lounge.
>
> She has danced occasionally.... She has not gone out very much, but has read almost constantly, having a book with her at meals. On only one occasion has she breakfasted in the dining-room. On other days she has breakfasted in her room, but has always appeared for luncheon and has eaten heartily.[8]

According to the *Harrogate Advertiser*:

> During her stay she acted as an ordinary guest and took part in the dancing and singing at the Sunday evening concert. She even tried to dance the Charleston with an elderly partaker but did not appear to know the steps.
>
> She conversed freely with the other guests and gave them to understand she had been in Torquay [It was true that, after the death of her mother that April, Agatha had visited Torquay, her home town, where she had spent her childhood]. It was presumed that she had left the bulk of her luggage there or in store. She talked in a perfectly rational manner and nothing in her speech or manner aroused any suspicions.
>
> She visited places of entertainment with friends she made in the hotel, and took walks around the town. It is stated that she purchased many books of detective fiction, and that she was a great reader of newspapers... but her chief interest was in crossword puzzles.[9]
>
> [Mrs Neele] was very musical, and often accompanied herself on the piano in the lounge. Many songs she sang without music and she was particularly fond of Devonshire songs. She asked the vocalist at the Sunday-night concert to sing 'Glorious Devon'. Her contribution to the programme on that occasion was, 'Softly awakes my Heart' from 'Samson and Delilah' which she sang in French, in a light soprano voice.[10]

On Saturday, 11 December 1926, eight days after Mrs Neele's arrival at The Hydro, the following advertisement appeared in The Times newspaper.

FRIENDS and RELATIVES of TERESA NEELE, late of South Africa, please COMMUNICATE.—Write Box R.702, The Times, EC4.[11]

According to the *Harrogate Herald*, during her stay in Harrogate, 'Mrs Neele' had:

been in and out of the Hydro as an ordinary guest, but had not, so far as had been observed, done any writing or acted in any way which might lead her fellow guests to suspect she was the lady for whom the Surrey Police had been searching so ardently. It is believed that she visited the Royal Baths on Thursday [9 December], and that Mr F. J. C. Broome, the General Manager, had his suspicions.[12]

As time went by, however, it gradually dawned upon the hotel's staff, guests, and in particular, members of the dance band who regularly entertained at The Hydro, that as far as Mrs Neele was concerned, all was not what it seemed. To the *Daily Mail*, Mr Taylor, Manager of the hotel declared:

What account of herself she gave to them [the other guests] I cannot tell you, but although I understand they remarked several times to each other on the resemblance between their fellow-guest and the missing woman, they did not really believe she could be Mrs Christie. Whether they remarked about it to her I do not know.

This morning, however [Tuesday 14 December], my wife, whose original suspicions still remained active, compared Mrs Christie's appearance once more with the photograph published. This time she made up her mind and the Harrogate police were informed. They sent up to the Hydro and telephoned to the Guildford police. Colonel Christie was informed, and arrived here this evening.

Also to the *Daily Mail*, Mrs Taylor, Manageress of The Hydro, admitted that:

for some time she had thought the woman staying at the hotel resembled photographs of Mrs Christie. She said: 'I am glad everything has turned out all right, because I took on a certain responsibility in not informing the police. Someone outside the hotel informed the police, although some of the servants here had said that there seemed to be a great resemblance between the woman and the pictures. I told them to say nothing. She was quite normal and happy and acted quite as an ordinary visitor. She did not give any suggestion of her identity, and I think she must have lost her memory.[13]

According to Gwen Robyns:

The Harry Codd Hydro Dance Band—known to residents as the Happy Hydro Boys [played] in the evenings in the Palm Lounge. Dressed in their neat dinner jackets, their hit tunes at the time were 'Yes, We Have No Bananas' and 'Don't Bring Lulu', suitable accompaniments for the Charleston, which was all the rage.[14]

The *Harrogate Advertiser* reported that Mr. R. H. ('Bob') Tappin and Mr. Robert W. Leeming, both members of the dance band:

were both attracted to her [Mrs Neele] by her awkward manner, even on the day of her arrival, but did not become suspicious until a week later.[15]

In an interview, Mr Tappin, who plays the banjo in the band and also sings at the Sunday concerts, said that on the night of Saturday 4 December, he noticed Mrs Christie in the ballroom. 'There was something about her which made her stand out apart from the other guests. Her dress and her demeanour were different, and she seemed rather awkward. I was particularly interested in the case because I come from the neighbourhood of Newlands Corner.

On Sunday [5 December], at the social function in the lounge, she sang something from Samson and Delilah, and I noticed a strong resemblance to Mrs Christie. Again on the following Saturday [11 December], when we were playing, I saw her and was more impressed because I had in the meantime studied all the photographs I could get hold of.

On Sunday [12 December] I was singing at the concert and she was also singing. I sat next to her and studied her as much as I could. One of the songs she sang was 'Softly awakes my heart' in French. She also sang a song to her own accompaniment, which greatly impressed me, because she appeared to know it thoroughly although she had no music. The song was 'I once loved a boy, a bonny, bonny boy'.

She then asked me if I would sing 'Glorious Devon', and that to me was an important point, because she came from the South and might have a special liking for south country songs. She also asked for 'Up from Somerset'. I gave this and also 'Drake goes West', and she seemed thoroughly to enjoy them. Mrs Christie, who sang most of the songs to her own accompaniment, tried another song, lent her by Miss Corbett, the lady entertainer, but she broke down and laughingly said she did not know it.[16]

When I went home I said to Bob Leeming, who is with me in the band [in which he played the saxophone], that the likeness to Mrs Christie was very marked. He had also noticed it, and we got out all the papers and studied the photographs and were then so sure of the fact that we decided to inform the police of our suspicions. It was a foul night, but we turned out at 11 o'clock,[17] and went to the police station, where we told the officer-in-charge what we felt. In the morning [of Monday 13 December] Detective-Sgt Baldwin [of the Harrogate Constabulary] had a talk to us, and the rest you know.

Leeming said he:

thought Mrs Christie [if indeed it was her] seemed an eccentric. We watched as much as we could, and she seemed rather awkward. We studied the photographs, and last Sunday my wife and I were at the Tappins and the mystery was the sole topic of our conversation. Mrs Leeming [Leeming's wife] strongly urged us to go to the police, but we hesitated, feeling that we might be making ourselves a laughing stock. However, we did go and, of course, it has turned out as we thought.[18]

The outcome was that, following this tip off by Leeming and Tappin:

Supt McDowall [sometimes spelt 'MacDowell', of the Harrogate Police], along with Inspector Hellewell and Detective-Sergeant Baldwin, visited the Hydro, and unobtrusively watched the lady. There was sufficient likeness to warrant Supt McDowall getting in touch with Supt Kenward of the Surrey police.[19]

Gwen Robyns, who was personally acquainted with Superintendent Kenward's daughter Gladys Dobson, confirms that it was during the evening of Monday 13 December that the Harrogate police:

sent a message to Deputy Chief Constable Kenward of the Surrey police [stating] that they had every reason to believe that the missing woman had been living in that area [i.e. of Harrogate] since her disappearance.[20]

Superintendent Kenward, however, for reasons best known to himself, remained unconvinced, and therefore chose not to apprise Archie of the news. Said Gwen Robyns:

Persisting in his belief that the body—dead or alive—would be found within 40 miles of Newlands Corner, Kenward decided not to take any action on the Harrogate police's message and not to advise Colonel Christie.

On the following morning [Tuesday 14 December] the Harrogate police were again on the telephone, and so insistent that their theory was right that Kenward decided to change his plans.[21]

It was just after 9 a.m. on Tuesday December 14 that Deputy Chief Constable Kenward tried to telephone Colonel Christie at his home, Styles, [i.e. with the news of Agatha's discovery] and was told that the Colonel had just left for his office in London.

Meanwhile, it fell to the Surrey Constabulary to break the news to Carlo that Agatha had been found. Said the *Daily Mail's* special correspondent:

The Harrogate news was telephoned to Mrs Christie's home by the Surrey police just after noon today [Wednesday 15 December]. Miss Fisher told me this evening: 'I could not go [to Harrogate] because of leaving Rosalind: therefore I telephoned Col. Christie at his place of business in London and he arranged to go by the 1.40 train' [from London's King's Cross Station, which was scheduled to arrive at Harrogate at 6.10 p.m.[22]]

At 6.30 to-night Col. Christie identified his wife at Harrogate Hydro, where she had been staying since the day after her disappearance under an assumed name.

To avoid frightening Mrs Christie, the Colonel, with Superintendent McDowall and other officers of the Harrogate police, hid near the hotel lift, which stands by the broad staircase leading down to the dining-room.

When Mrs Christie, who was dressed in an evening gown, came down the steps, her husband nodded to the police officers, who informed her that the colonel was there. Later Col. and Mrs Christie had dinner together.

Superintendent McDowall made the following statement to-night: 'We first obtained information yesterday afternoon [Tuesday 14 December] and thought it was of sufficient importance to make inquiries.

This was presumably when, having placed 'Mrs Neele' under surveillance, the police had satisfied themselves that this lady was, in fact, Mrs Christie.

Today we sent for Col. Christie, and he arrived here tonight and identified the woman as his wife.[23]

Tonight, [Wednesday 15 December] when Col. Christie arrived, there were about twenty-five newspaper men waiting in the hall of the Hydro. He was shown the visitors' book which his wife had signed, and he recognised her handwriting. I understand that Mrs Christie remarked on her husband looking nervous.

It is stated that after dinner she introduced the colonel to a visitor as her brother. She has always taken a morning and evening paper. Tonight she read a paper in which was the headline, 'Mrs Christie, the novelist, said to be in a Harrogate hydro.' I am told that it did not appear to convey anything to her. Most people say that Mrs Christie has appeared to be perfectly normal.

Col. and Mrs Christie have tonight, I understand, engaged a small private suite. They are expected to leave the Hydro early tomorrow and go south.[24]

A statement which Mr Taylor made to the Press Association was quoted by the *Daily Mail* as follows:

The meeting between husband and wife in the lounge of the Hydro was pathetic. Mrs Christie approached and took up a copy of an evening paper which contained a story of the searches for herself and a photograph of her.

The husband immediately recognised his wife, but she only seemed to regard him as an acquaintance whose identity she could not quite fix. It was sufficient, however, to permit of her accompanying her husband to the dining-room, where they had dinner together.[25]

According to the *Harrogate Herald:*

Col. Christie arrived in Harrogate by train shortly after six o'clock. He was unaccompanied and was not met at the station. He walked out of the station, and after traversing several streets asked a policeman to direct him to the police station. Here he was seen by Supt McDowall, and the two proceeded by car to the Hydro. They took up a position in the lounge and Col. Christie was obviously labouring under great strain. Mrs Christie was dressing for dinner, and they had over half an hour to wait before she put in an appearance. She walked down the stairs instead of the lift, and when Col. Christie saw her, he turned to Supt McDowall and said she was his wife. There was an affectionate meeting, and immediately afterwards the two went into the dining-room for dinner. Mrs Christie was attired in salmon pink nulon.[26]

On Tuesday evening, *the Daily Mail* reported as follows:

Colonel Christie said, 'There is no question about the identity. It is my wife. She has suffered from the most complete loss of memory, and I do not think she knows who she is. She does not know me and she does not know where she is. I am hoping that rest and quiet will restore her. I am hoping to take her to London tomorrow to see a doctor and specialist.' Colonel Christie expressed his thanks to the police.[27]

* * *

When Agatha checked in at The Hydro, she had registered under the surname of 'Neele'. But why? Surely, it was no coincidence that this was also the surname of Archie's mistress Nancy Neele.

By all accounts she blended in with the other guests; made friends; joined in with the entertainments, and enjoyed her meals. But what possessed her to put an advertisement in *The*

Times under the name 'Teresa Neele' when this person did not actually exist, and therefore could not have had any 'friends or relatives'?

According to Laura Thompson, Archie told the Daily Mail that in his opinion, Agatha had:

inserted the advertisement in *The Times* under the name of Neele, asking her relatives to communicate, because she was in the extraordinary position of being in a strange hotel for no purpose that she could think of and with no knowledge of who she was other than the conviction that Teresa Neele was her real name. The doctors told me that such an action was compatible with the action of a person suffering from loss of memory.[28]

Meanwhile, Gwen Robyns described how, in London during the week prior to her disappearance:

when she had clearly been Mrs Agatha Christie, she had lost a diamond ring at Harrods [the London department store in Knightsbridge]. When she realised this, she wrote to the store from Harrogate describing the ring and asking that it be forwarded to Mrs Teresa Neele, giving the address of the hotel at Harrogate [The Hydro]. And the store did.[29]

Laura Thompson gave a slightly different account of events. Agatha, having visited the Army and Navy stores:

took a taxi to Harrods. In the ground-floor Jewellery Department she left a ring to be repaired, giving her name and address for it as Mrs Neele, The Harrogate Hydro.[30]

According to Janet Morgan, Agatha also took a taxi to Whiteley's Department Store, Bayswater, one and a half miles north-west of Harrods in the W2 district of London.[31]

Band member Bob Tappin, commented on Mrs Neele's 'different' dress and demeanour; Robert Leeming found her to be 'eccentric'; both described her as being 'rather awkward' (presumably in her manner). According to Archie, she knew neither who she was nor where she was. But most bizarre of all, was Agatha's reaction when she was reunited with her husband, whom she mistook, according to one account, for her brother, and according to another, for 'an acquaintance'.

Laura Thompson opined that at Harrogate, Agatha was not her normal self. '...she was not here, Mrs Christie was not here. Here instead was a ghost who walked through the Valley Gardens, looking up to the stone buildings that rose behind the trees.'[32] However, does this provide anything like an adequate explanation of Agatha's behaviour? Surely not.

Finally, it was Laura's view that:

Something of the mystery will always remain. The blank face of the quarry [chalk pit] will never give up all its secrets. The facts may now be known and much of the intention behind them, but in the end what is left is a story. A mystery story. Her finest, because it cannot be solved. Questions can be asked. Did she plan it all? Did she lose her memory? Was it a publicity stunt? Was she after revenge, or pity, or an end to it all?[33]

CHAPTER 6

Aftermath

The *Daily Mail's* special correspondent revealed that he, himself:

> was the first person to convey the definite news of Mrs Christie's discovery to Styles, her home, from which she disappeared last Friday week.
>
> Miss Fisher, her secretary, who had been anxiously awaiting a telephone message from the police— which did not come for some time—was delighted. 'Thank God for that,' was her first remark. 'It is splendid. I felt that it must be so because I could not believe anything else, although there were moments when I did not know what to believe in view of the letter I received. That letter gave us no idea where she might have gone. I do not wish to discuss it now. There is really no reason, for it was a personal letter, and only told us that she felt she must leave this house.'
>
> Little Rosalind, the eight-year-old daughter of Mrs Christie [Rosalind was, in fact, aged seven at the time], was in bed when I conveyed the news. She has never been told of her mother's disappearance, and now will never know.[1]

(According to Gwen Robyns, 'Rosalind had been told that her mother was away writing a book, a state of affairs with which she was familiar and accepted.'[2])

The Times reported, that on Wednesday 15 December, Agatha, accompanied by her husband Archie, was taken to Abney Hall, Cheadle, the residence of her brother-in-law James Watts 'who is a member of the firm of S. and J. Watts Limited, merchants, of Manchester'.[3] Agatha, in her autobiography, described James as 'the one person who was entirely on my side, and reassured me in all that I was doing...'.[4]

> Mr and Mrs Watts arrived at Harrogate early yesterday morning and left the hotel with Colonel and Mrs Christie by a back door for the station. They entered a London train and changed at Leeds for Manchester. Mrs Christie locked herself in the compartment with Mrs Watts, Colonel Christie and Mr Watts remaining on guard outside till just before the train left. At Manchester all four entered a motor-car and drove to Abney Hall, where the gates were locked after their arrival.[5]
>
> Colonel Christie would not allow his wife to be questioned, and said that she had completely lost her memory and was 'very ill indeed'.

The account given by the *Harrogate Advertiser* described how, when the party had arrived at Harrogate railway station:

instead of going onto the platform in the ordinary way, they were led through another entrance just as the train steamed into the station. A first-class compartment had been reserved for them, and they immediately took their seats and pulled down all the blinds. Mrs Christie was attired in a two-piece suit of rose pink material, with a hat to match, and she wore a string of pearls. She was chatting gaily with her husband during the short wait in the station. The door of the compartment was closely guarded by a friend against the army of press men and photographers.[6]

The *Daily Mail* claimed that one of its reporters:

was the first person last night [Tuesday 15 December] to convey to Mrs Helmsley, the mother-in-law of Mrs Agatha Christie, at her home at Dorking, the news that her daughter-in-law had been found safe and sound. 'No!' exclaimed Mrs Hemlsley, falling back against the wall. 'I cannot believe it.' When the truth of the statement was impressed upon her she said: 'Oh! how poor Agatha must have suffered! Her mind must have been a complete blank. Even now I cannot really think she can be alive.'

Mrs Helmsley then expressed the opinion that this was a case of amnesia. (Impaired ability to learn new information or inability to recall previously learned information or past events.)[7]

I know her so well that I refuse to believe that she did not lose her memory. She would not live in an hotel on her own, fully alive to all the fuss and anxiety she was causing, not sending a word even to her own relatives. She must have had a terrible shock on seeing Archie in the hotel, which probably restored her mental balance.[8]

In fact, from her subsequent behaviour, it was clear that Agatha's mental balance had not been completely restored. In a subsequent interview with the *Daily Mail*, Mrs Helmsley revealed, in reference to Agatha's visit to her on the morning of her disappearance, that:

while waiting for the kettle to boil she sang a few songs and joked with Rosalind, and I remarked to her that she seemed much better. 'Yes,' she replied, 'I do.' But a few minutes later she seemed to become depressed again.[9]

And when Mrs Helmsley remarked to Agatha that she 'was not wearing her wedding ring this day but only her engagement ring', Agatha had:

sat perfectly still for some time, gazing into space, and giving a hysterical laugh... [Then she] turned away and patted Rosalind's head. I am inclined to think that my daughter-in-law planned her end and deliberately drove the car to where it was found. She knew the roads so well and even in the dark she would not lose her way. [However] Although physically strong she could never crank up a car if it had stopped.

She was devoted to her husband and child and would never willingly have left them. It is my opinion that in a fit of depression, and not knowing where she was going or what she was doing, my daughter-in-law abandoned her car at Newlands Corner and wandered away over the Downs.[10]

On Thursday 16 December, Archie made the following statement to *The Times*:

> My wife is extremely ill, suffering from complete loss of memory. Three years have dropped out of her life. She cannot recall anything that has happened during that period. The fact that she lives at Sunningdale has no significance for her, and she does not seem to realize that her home is at The Styles. As to what has happened since she left there, her mind is a complete blank. She has not the slightest recollection of going to Newlands Corner or of proceeding eventually to Harrogate. As was only to be expected, she is very much upset as the result of the journey yesterday, and has no idea what all the fuss is about. She now knows who I am, and has also realized that Mrs Watts is her sister. It is somewhat remarkable that she does not know she has a daughter. In this connection, when she was shown a picture of herself and Rosalind, her little daughter, she asked who the child was, 'What is the child like?' and 'How old is she?'
>
> My wife has been seen today by a local doctor, and this afternoon a specialist is coming over from Manchester for a further consultation. I tell you this in order that you will respect my feelings and not worry the specialist or myself. All the worry has been terrible, and all we want now is peace and quietness. I have been offered £500 to tell how my wife came to Harrogate. I do not know, and she cannot tell me.[11]

The doctors in question were Henry Wilson, MRCS (the Watts' family doctor), and Donald Core MD,[12] a lecturer in nervous diseases from Manchester University. On 16 December 1926 they issued this joint statement:

> After careful examination of Mrs Agatha Christie this afternoon, we have formed the opinion that she is suffering from an unquestionably genuine loss of memory and that for her future welfare she should be spared all anxiety and excitement.[13]

On Wednesday 22 December, Archie brought Rosalind to Abney Hall to be reunited with her mother,[14] but the outcome of this meeting was far from satisfactory.

> She [Rosalind] recalled going with her governess [Carlo] to her aunt's home in Cheshire, Abney Hall, where her mother went to stay after she was found, and finding that 'she did not remember anything we had been doing together or even the stories she used to tell me'.[15]

According to Laura Thompson:

> It was said that Agatha did not recognise her daughter when she saw her again at Abney. This is impossible to believe, although it is very easy to imagine Agatha pretending to do such a thing.[16]

To a lay person this may, perhaps, appear to be the case, but to a psychiatrist such as Dr Anthony Storr of Oxford University, there was the possibly of a quite different explanation, as will be seen.

Meanwhile, Robert Leeming was given a silver cigarette case, inscribed with the words 'With our best wishes, Colonel & Mrs Christie'.[17] The other members of the band were each given a silver propelling pencil.[18]

On 20 April 1928, Agatha was granted a decree nisi on the grounds of her husband's 'adultery with a woman unknown at the Grosvenor Hotel, Victoria in November 1927'. Agatha was also granted custody of Rosalind, and the costs of the case.[19] Agatha's divorce was made absolute on 29 October 1928. In December, Archie married Nancy Neele. The couple subsequently had a son, Archie junior.

* * *

Archie's mother-in-law, Mrs Helmsley, noticed, on the morning of Agatha's disappearance, that her behaviour was abnormal and that she was depressed. Following her discovery, Archie declared that Agatha was suffering from 'complete loss of memory'. What was particularly disturbing was that she failed to recognize a photograph of her daughter Rosalind, and appeared not to know what Rosalind was like nor how old she was. And when she and Rosalind were finally reunited, Agatha had no memory of their past lives together. Can Agatha's behaviour be explained simply by loss of memory, or was there more to it than that? This will be discussed shortly.

CHAPTER 7

Agatha's Own Account of her Disappearance

Two years later, on 16 February 1928, Agatha, her memory having recovered somewhat, made a statement to the *Daily Mail*. She was prompted to do this as the result of a court case (which did not directly concern her) in which Mitchell Hedges, an explorer, claimed damages for alleged libel from the *Daily Express*.[1] In the action, Agatha's name was mentioned, and her disappearance was described by Hedges as 'a foolish hoax on the police'—a hoax being defined as 'a humorous or malicious deception'.[2]) This prompted the following response from Agatha.

I thought everybody had forgotten about the affair, but the reference in the libel suit shows how many people still think I deliberately disappeared.

Of course I know that at the time a large number of people thought that I had gone away to seek publicity, to carry out a stupid hoax, or to have a subtle revenge on somebody.

What actually happened was this. I left home that night [Friday 3 December] in a state of high nervous strain with the intention of doing something desperate. I drove in my car over the crest of the Downs in the direction of a quarry. The car struck something and I was flung against the steering wheel and injured my chest and head.

I was dazed by the blow and lost my memory. For 24 hours [during Saturday morning and early afternoon, to be more accurate] I wandered in a dream and then found myself at Harrogate—a well-contented and perfectly happy woman who believed she had just come from South Africa.

The trouble really began with the death of my mother in the spring of 1926. That affected me very deeply, and on top of this shock there came a number of private troubles, into which I would rather not enter. Instead of sleeping well, as I had done previously, I began to suffer from insomnia, and slept on the average only two hours a night.

On the day of my disappearance I drove over, in the afternoon, to Dorking with my daughter to see a relative [her mother-in-law Mrs Helmsley]. I was at this time in a very despondent state of mind. I just wanted my life to end. As I passed by Newlands Corner that afternoon I saw a quarry, and there came into my mind a thought of driving into it. However, as my daughter was with me in the car, I dismissed the idea at once.

That night I felt terribly miserable. I felt that I could go on no longer. I left home at 10 o'clock in my car with a few articles of clothing in a suitcase and about £60 in my bag. I had drawn some money from the bank shortly before as I had decided to go that winter to South Africa with my daughter, and I wanted to make preparations.

All that night I drove aimlessly about. In my mind there was the vague idea of ending everything. I drove automatically down roads I knew, but without thinking where I was going. As far as I remember I went to London and drove to Euston Station. Why I went there I do not know.

Had Agatha mistaken Euston, the terminus for trains to the West Midlands and the North-West, for King's Cross, the terminus for the North-East, including Harrogate?

> I believe I then drove out to Maidenhead [in Surrey], where I looked at the river. I thought about jumping in, but realized that I could swim too well to drown. I then drove back to London again, and then on to Sunningdale [but apparently, she did not call in at Styles]. From there I went on to Newlands Corner.
>
> When I reached a point on the road which I thought was near the quarry I had seen in the afternoon, I turned the car off the road down the hill towards it. I left [i.e. let go] the wheel and let the car run. The car struck something with a jerk and pulled up suddenly. I was flung against the steering wheel and my head hit something.

In other words, Agatha drove along the A25, up to the top of Merrow Downs to Newlands Corner, to where Trodds Lane joins the road from the west side. Almost immediately came a right fork into Water Lane, when the car would have begun the steep, 600-yard descent of Albury Downs. Now came a sharp right-hand bend, where Agatha would have had to slow down in order to negotiate it. From here to the chalk pit was another 100 yards or so, downhill.

> Up to this moment I was Mrs Christie. I was certainly in an abnormal state of mind, and scarcely knew what I was doing or where I was going. All the same I knew I was Mrs Christie. After the accident in the car, however, I lost my memory. For 24 hours after the accident my mind was an almost complete blank. Since I recovered my health I have managed to recall a little of what happened in those 24 hours.
>
> I remember arriving at a big railway station and asking what it was, and being surprised to learn it was Waterloo. It is strange that the railway authorities there did not recall [i.e. apprehend or detain] me, as I was covered with mud and I had smeared blood on my face from a cut on my hand. I could never make out how this cut had been caused.
>
> I believe I wandered about London and I then remember arriving at the hotel in Harrogate. I was still muddy and showing signs of my accident when I arrived there. I had now become, in my mind, Mrs Tessa [Teresa] Neele of South Africa.
>
> I can quite understand why I went to Harrogate. The motor-car accident brought on neuritis, and once before in my life I had thought of going to Harrogate to have treatment for this complaint.
>
> While I was at Harrogate I had treatment regularly. The only thing which really puzzled me was the fact that I had scarcely any luggage with me. I could not quite make this out. I had not even a toothbrush in my case, and I wondered why I had come there without one.
>
> I realised, of course, that I had been in some kind of accident. I had a severe bruise on my chest, and my head was also bruised. As Mrs Neele I was very happy and contented. I had become, as it were, a new woman, and all the worries and anxieties of Mrs Christie had left me. When I was brought back to my life as Mrs Christie again many of my worries and anxieties returned, and although I am now quite well and cheerful, and have lost my old morbid tendencies completely, I have not quite that utter happiness of Mrs Neele.
>
> At Harrogate I read every day about Mrs Christie's disappearance and came to the conclusion that she was dead. I regarded her as having acted stupidly. I was greatly struck by my resemblance to her and pointed it out to other people in the hotel. It never occurred to me that I might be her, as I was quite

satisfied in my mind as to who I was. I thought I was a widow, and that I had a son who had died, for I had in my bag a photograph of my little girl when very young with the name 'Teddy' upon it. I even tried to obtain a book by this Mrs Christie to read.

When I was finally discovered it was not for some time that doctors and relatives restored in my mind memories of my life as Mrs Christie. These memories were drawn from my subconscious mind slowly.

First, I recalled my childhood days and thought of relatives and friends as they were when children. By gradual steps I recalled later and later episodes in my life until I could remember what happened just before the motor accident.

The doctors even made me try to recall the events in the blank 24 hours afterwards, as they said that for the health of my mind there should be no hiatus of any kind in my recollections. That is why I can now recall, at the same time, my existence as Mrs Christie and as Mrs Neele.[3]

* * *

What was Agatha's objective in driving to London? Surely one would only visit Euston Station in order a) to catch a train, b) to check-up on the times of trains to the West Midlands and the North-West, or c) to meet a friend or relative. Was her car crash at Newlands Corner the result of a genuine suicide attempt? Why did she travel to Harrogate, in particular (for which the terminus was King's Cross, not Euston)? And most curiously of all, what caused her metamorphosis from Agatha into the new persona of 'Mrs Teresa Neele'?

Laura Thompson appears to dismiss Agatha's account of her night-time journey. Instead she states, with no corroborative evidence, that Agatha drove from Styles to Bagshot, Woking, Guildford, Albury, Chilworth, Godalming, and almost to Hurstmore Cottage, before arriving at Newlands Corner,[4] where she fell asleep in her car.

CHAPTER 8

Gwen Robyns and her Interview with Gladys Dobson (née Kenward)

In her book *The Mystery of Agatha Christie*, Gwen Robyns quotes Lord Ritchie Calder, who at the time of Agatha's disappearance was crime reporter for the *Daily News*, as saying:

> One thing that was established by press interrogation was that the secretary [Carlo], whether at Mrs Christie's suggestion or because she panicked, telephoned the country house at Godalming on the Friday night to warn Colonel Christie.

If Carlo did telephone Archie at Godalming, it could not have been at Agatha's behest, as by the time Carlo had returned from London, Agatha had already left Styles. It is possible, however, that having returned to Styles and discovered that Agatha had driven off into the night, Carlo put two and two together and reasoned that she may well have been on her way to confront Archie about his mistress. Alternatively, if such a telephone call did take place, it is possible that it was Agatha herself who made it, just prior to her leaving home.

Continued Calder:

> A dinner party was in progress. This was more than an assignation; it was what the household described as an 'engagement' party for Colonel Christie and Miss Neele.

This was a little premature, surely, considering that Archie was a married man.

> He was called from the table, took the call, made abrupt apologies and drove off in his car. The implication was that he was going to intercept her to avoid a confrontation at the house.[1]
> The Berkshire Police checked the times of both Colonel and Mrs Christie's departures and there is every reason to believe that they could, in fact, have met at Newlands Corner.

If so, then this, for Agatha, would have meant a journey of about fifteen miles, and for Archie, one of about five miles.

Assuming that such a meeting did take place (even though Agatha made no mention of it in her statement to the *Daily Mail*), and that Agatha had given Archie an ultimatum, to the effect that he must now choose between herself and Nancy Neele, and supposing the response from Archie had been that he wanted her to give him a divorce, in order that he could be free to marry Nancy, then this might explain why Agatha drove around for the remainder of the night in a state of mental turmoil, before returning to Newlands Corner, the scene of her last traumatic meeting with her husband, to make her suicide attempt.[2]

However, as already mentioned, Archie's host for the weekend, Sam James, categorically denied that any such meeting took place.

In 1978, Gwen Robyns travelled to 'a lonely farm cottage in the West Country' in order to interview Mrs Gladys Dobson, daughter of Superintendent Kenward, who was then aged 75.

In respect of the letters left behind or posted by Agatha prior to her disappearance, Gladys, who was aged 23 at the time in question, told Gwen that:

> Yes, there was a fourth letter [in addition to the ones left [by Agatha] for Archie and Carlo, and the one posted to Campbell Christie]. It was addressed to my father and marked 'private and confidential,' and posted on the Friday night that she went missing.

Larger provincial post offices were open from 8 a.m. to 7.30 p.m. or 8 p.m., and smaller provincial post offices from 9 a.m. to 7 p.m.[3] Therefore, Agatha must have posted her letter to Superintendent Kenward at some time prior to 8 p.m. at the very latest—i.e. well before she left Styles.

> He received it in the 10 a.m. mail on Saturday and brought it to our home nearby to show me before going over immediately to inform the Sunningdale police station and begin investigations. [Gladys may perhaps be forgiven for being ignorant of the fact that there was neither a police station nor a resident constable at Sunningdale at that time: the nearest station being at Ascot, just over 2 miles away.][4]

Why did Kenward show Agatha's letter to his daughter Gladys? This was because a) she acted as his 'confidential secretary, and b) he therefore knew that he could trust her to keep the matter confidential.[5]

Furthermore, said Gladys:

> The letter was from a woman who told how she feared for her life and that she was frightened what might happen to her. She was appealing for help. The signature on that letter was Agatha Christie.[6]
>
> When he retired my father ordered that all the personal correspondence about this case should be destroyed. I burned the copies of the letters, including the one Mrs Christie left her secretary should she have died.[7]

(By this, Gladys was presumably referring to transcripts of the letters, rather than to the actual letters concerned. The letter for Carlo, for example, which the police had taken charge of, was subsequently returned to Agatha's secretary, as already mentioned.)

This latter statement by Gladys, therefore implies that there may have been *a fifth* letter, left by Agatha for Carlo, which was only to be opened in the event of Agatha's death. However, what is not explained is how this alleged fifth letter came to be in the possession of Superintendent Kenward of the Surrey Constabulary, and not in that of the Berkshire Constabulary, under whose jurisdiction Sunningdale lay. Is it possible that Gladys was mistaken, or that she had concocted the story? The answer, on both counts, is, probably not. She had no motive for so doing, and according to Gwen Robyns, her:

> brain was crisp and her memory astonishing for a 75 year old. Many years of active service in the police force as her father's confidential secretary had seen to that.

Finally, said Gwen Robyns in 1978, Gladys Dobson:

> still has strong affiliations with the Surrey Constabulary, and each year she is the only woman guest at the reunion dinner to which she donates a trophy of a magnum of champagne. She is part of 'the old days'; the men love her and every year there is a get-together photograph taken with this diminutive woman seated in the front row, flanked by grinning retired police officers.[8]

So there is no way that Gladys would have wished to jeopardise the high esteem in which she was held by members of the Berkshire Constabulary, some of whom had been colleagues of her late husband, by giving false information.

Further evidence in support of the fact that Agatha did indeed communicate with the police—i.e. Superintendent Kenward—and express a fear that she might be murdered was provided by Kenward's report to the Home Office, in which he stated as follows:

> In conclusion, may I reiterate that the lady disappeared under circumstances which opened out all sorts of possibilities—she might have been wandering with loss of memory over that vast open country around Newlands Corner, or she might have fallen down one of the numerous gravel pits that abound there and are covered in most instances with undergrowth and lying helpless in agony, or she might have been, as was strongly suggested to the police, the victim of a serious crime.[9]

In the same Home Office report, it was said of Kenward that:

> he does not think they would have troubled even to this extent [i.e. with the search] had it not been for communications alleging murder, of which [the] police had to take a certain amount of notice.[10]

It is hardly surprising, therefore, that Agatha's letter to Kenward led him to believe that Agatha had been murdered, presumably having been abducted from her car at Newlands Corner, and this explains why he persisted with the search in the vicinity of Newlands Corner. As Kenward himself said in a subsequent letter to the Home Office:

> The circumstances fully justified me in taking the action that I did. As for prosecuting enquiries in other parts of the country, that was entirely a matter for the Berkshire Police, from whose district Mrs Christie disappeared.[11]

But the superintendent must have wondered a) why Agatha had contacted him, instead of the Berkshire police, within in whose jurisdiction her home at Sunningdale lay, and b) why, having done so, she had opted to write a letter, rather than to visit him at the Guildford Police Headquarters and voice her fears to him in person.

CHAPTER 9

Making Sense of Agatha's Seemingly Confusing Letters

First, it should be pointed out, that all the letters left behind by Agatha or posted by her after her disappearance, are believed to have been written by her at Styles, and signed by her using her own name.

The first letter to Carlo

Agatha told Carlo that 'in the circumstances [she] did not believe she could go to Yorkshire',[1] and she therefore instructed her secretary to cancel her weekend reservation at the hotel in Beverley. Had Archie originally agreed to accompany Agatha to Beverley, and then pulled out, as Jared Cade suggested?[2] And was this why Agatha instructed that the hotel booking be cancelled? This is a distinct possibility.

The second letter to Carlo

As already mentioned, Superintendent Kenward's daughter Gladys Dobson, told Gwen Robyns:

> I burned the copies of the letters, including the one Mrs Christie left her secretary should she have died.[3]

This, therefore implies that Agatha left a second letter for Carlo, one which was only to be opened in the event of her death.

The letter ('note') to Archie

Although the contents of the letter that Agatha left for her husband will probably never be known, according to Archie it shed no light on Agatha's intentions in respect of her intended destination. Therefore, all Archie knew was what he had learned from Carlo—i.e. that Agatha had changed her mind and no longer intended to visit Yorkshire.

The letter to Superintendent Kenward of the Surrey Constabulary

According to Kenward's daughter Gladys Dobson, the letter from Agatha to her father 'told how she feared for her life and that she was frightened what might happen to her. She was appealing for help'.[4] The conclusion must be, therefore, that Agatha wished to apprise Superintendent Kenward of the fact that some dramatic event was shortly due to take place in Surrey, the county of Kenward's jurisdiction—rather than in Berkshire, in which county her home town of Sunningdale was situated. Kenward appears to have interpreted this to mean that Agatha feared that her husband Archie might murder her [for refusing to grant him a divorce]. But the question is, how was it possible for Archie to murder Agatha when he was at Godalming, spending the weekend with his mistress? Or did the letter have a quite different meaning, and did Agatha really mean that she was frightened that she might be tempted to take her own life?

Also, when Agatha posted her 'letter of desperation' to Kenward on the Friday night, she must have realised that his first thought, on receiving it next morning, would be to contact her (or to ask his colleagues from the Berkshire Constabulary to do so) a) to check on her safety, and b) to investigate the matter further. But having already decided to leave home, Agatha had arranged matters in such a way that he would be unable to do so. So why send Kenward the letter in the first place?

The letter to Campbell Christie

As already mentioned, *The Times* newspaper reported that on Tuesday 7 December (i.e. seven days prior to Agatha being discovered at Harrogate), it was learned that Agatha's brother-in-law Campbell Christie, had received a letter from Agatha.[5] According to Janet Morgan, the letter was postmarked 'London SW 9.45 [a.m., Saturday] December 4'.[6] *The Times*, however, was more specific, and gave the postal district as 'SW1'.[7]

As already mentioned, the evidence indicates that Agatha arrived at London's Waterloo Station at some time between 8.25 a.m. and 9.01 a.m. that Saturday morning. According to Laura Thompson, she then 'took a taxi to the Army and Navy Stores [Victoria Street]. Before going in she posted her letter. It was addressed from Styles to her brother-in-law Campbell Christie…'.[8] This proposition by Laura makes sense: Victoria Street being situated across the River Thames from Waterloo Station, and in the SW1 district of London. This is therefore a district through which Agatha would have passed, having crossed Waterloo Bridge. (Incidentally, Nan Kon's residence at Chelsea Park Gardens was in the SW3 postal district of London, which is immediately adjacent to SW1.) Agatha, as already mentioned, must have composed this letter before she left Styles late the previous evening.

According to *The Times*, in the letter to Campbell, Agatha stated that she 'was in ill health and was going to a Yorkshire spa'.[9] The question therefore arises, why did she tell Carlo one thing—that she 'did not believe she could go to Yorkshire', and yet tell Campbell the opposite—that Yorkshire was, indeed, her destination? This, presumably, was because it was Agatha's intention to keep Carlo in the dark about her future movements (and also Archie, whom she knew would surely interrogate her secretary on his return from Godalming), whilst at the same time confiding her true intentions to Campbell, whom she once described as 'a great friend', 'a kind and lovable person',[10] and therefore someone who she knew would not betray her. But how does this tie in with her suicide attempt?

The likely sequence of events was as follows. At Styles on the Friday evening, Agatha felt suicidal and had it in mind to take her own life, and she presumably intended to do the deed at Newlands Corner, in the adjacent county of Surrey. She therefore wrote a letter to Superintendent Kenward of the Surrey Constabulary, voicing her fears to him in this regard, and put the letter in the post. She then had second thoughts, and decided to go to Yorkshire as originally intended (but not to Beverley). She therefore composed a letter to her brother-in-law Campbell Christie to this effect, to be posted the following day. However, in the meantime, she wished to keep this information from Carlo, for fear that her secretary would be interrogated by Archie, who would then pursue her. She also left another letter for Carlo, which was only to be opened in the event of her death—which suggests that the idea of suicide was still lurking in the back of her mind. She left a third letter, for her husband Archie, the contents of which are not known, as he destroyed it.

Agatha set off in her car at about 10 p.m., and headed towards London. However, during the course of the car journey, she became increasingly depressed and desperate. Finally, exhausted after a night of driving around in circles, she headed for Newlands Corner where she attempted to commit suicide. When the attempt failed, she made her way to London, en route to Harrogate, having now changed her mind yet again. In London, she posted the letter to Campbell which she had previously written to him.

According to Laura Thompson, Agatha anticipated that 'Campbell would read her letter; telephone Styles, and everything would be alright.'[11] In other words, he would apprise Archie of the fact that Agatha was paying a visit to a Yorkshire spa, and Archie would then come looking for his wife, having guessed that Harrogate was 'the likeliest place' for him to look. The news would also filter through to Carlo who would be reassured that her mistress 'was not dead after all'.[12]

CHAPTER 10

The Background to Agatha's Disappearance: Her Autobiography

Agatha's autobiography was published in 1977, the year after her death. Does it contain any clues as to the reason for her disappearance?

Agatha Mary Clarissa Miller (who became Agatha Christie), was born on 15 September 1890 at the coastal resort of Torquay in South Devonshire, which is where she spent her childhood. Her mother was Clarissa ('Clara'), whose family came from Sussex; and her father was Frederick Alvah Miller, an American who had moved to Manchester. At the time of their marriage, in April 1878, Frederick was aged 32 and Clara 24.

The couple set up home in Torquay, and it was here, in 1879, that Agatha's sister Margaret—'Madge'—was born. Soon afterwards, the couple relocated to the USA, where, in 1880, Agatha's brother Louis Montant—'Monty'—was born. Finally, the family returned to Torquay, having decided to reside there on a permanent basis.[1]

Using money which she had inherited as a legacy, Clara promptly purchased 'Ashfield'[2] in Barton Road, a sizeable property with extensive gardens, an orchard, conservatories, a tennis court, and a croquet lawn.[3] This is the house where Agatha was born, and around which her early life was centred.

Agatha began her autobiography by declaring that one of the most fortunate things that can happen to a person in their lifetime, was to have a happy childhood. Her own childhood, she described as being 'very happy'. She loved her home and her garden; her nanny was 'wise and patient', and her parents were 'two people who loved each other dearly and made a success of their marriage and of being parents'.[4]

Agatha described her mother Clara as someone who had a habit of seeing the world as a drama, or even as a melodrama, and because of the creative nature of her imagination, she was never able to visualise places or events as being 'drab or ordinary'. She was also highly intuitive, which meant that she was often able to deduce the thoughts of others.[5] It seems likely, therefore, that Agatha's own imaginativeness and creativity was largely inherited from her mother.

As for her father Frederick, she described him as a lazy man of independent means; a collector of fine furniture and china, glass and paintings, who spent the mornings and afternoons at his club, and, during the season, days at the cricket club—of which he was president. Nevertheless, Agatha acknowledged that Frederick had a loving nature, and was deeply concerned for his fellow men.[6] Also, Frederick possessed an extensive library, which included comprehensive editions of nineteenth-century novels. This facility would be of great benefit to Agatha in the years to come, in her own literary career.

In Agatha's early years, home and family were paramount, and it is, therefore, not surprising that she became deeply attached to those who were assigned to look after her. Agatha described her nurse/nanny as being elderly and rheumatic. Nonetheless, she was devoted to 'Nursie', with whom she shared so much.

For example, being allowed in the kitchen in order to help with the making of her own 'little cottage loaves and twists'. When Nursie retired, Agatha described this as 'the first real sorrow of my life'.[7] There was also a cook, Jane Rowe, who remained with the family for forty years, together with several housemaids and a parlourmaid. In this seemingly idyllic world, however, all was not entirely sweetness and light. It was when she was about five years old, recalled Agatha, that her father first began to have money worries.

Agatha's paternal grandfather, Nathaniel Miller, had invested in various trust funds, intended to provide an income for his relatives after his death. However, the money that was due to come to Agatha's father did not materialise—either because of 'sheer inefficiency', or because one of the four trustees had managed to manipulate matters to his own advantage.[8] It is therefore no coincidence that the plots of many of Agatha's future detective novels would revolve around the subject of stocks and shares, bonds, altered wills and the falsification of legal documents!

In order to economise, the Millers decided to let Ashfield and spend the winter of 1895 in France, where the cost of living was lower. Having crossed The Channel, Agatha described the excitement of going to bed in the train which would take them to Pau in the South of France, where they spent about six months. It was here that she went horse riding, and with the help of Marie Sijé—an assistant fitter whom the Christies met in the dressmaker's shop—improved her French. Soon Agatha was able not only to converse fluently, but also to read books in the French language. When Clara asked Marie if she would care to accompany the family back to England, the latter was delighted. Then they left for Paris, where they found the streets 'full of those new vehicles called *Automobiles*'.[9] They returned via Brittany and Guernsey.

These early experiences on the Continent would leave an indelible impression on Agatha; to the extent that she later chose to make her famous male detective a Belgian, Hercule Poirot, whose charm was that he could view the British, and particularly the English, with their traditions and eccentricities, from a continental standpoint.

Agatha's mother Clara was convinced that the best way to bring up girls was to give them as much freedom as possible, with good food and an abundance of fresh air. Their minds were not to be 'forced' in any way. Boys, of course, were an entirely different proposition. For them, education had to be along rigidly conventional lines. [10]

Clara also believed that children should not be permitted to read before they attained the age of eight years, as this was better, not only for their eyesight, but also for their minds. Despite this, Agatha had learnt to read by the age of five, which opened up 'the world of story books' to her from then onwards.[11]

During the Boer War, Agatha's brother Monty served with the Army in South Africa from 1899 to 1902, when he obtained a commission and relocated to India.

Agatha's father Frederick died on 26 November 1901, when she was aged 11. His health had gradually deteriorated, but despite this, no diagnosis had ever been made as to the exact nature of his illness.[12] Following this event, Agatha's mother Clara suffered a series of heart attacks. Agatha now became extremely anxious. She would wake at night, her heart pounding, certain that her mother had died. She acknowledged that she had always been 'over-burdened with imagination', and that this characteristic, which, in her view, was fundamental to the craft of the novelist, had been useful to her in her profession. However, the down side was that it could give a person of her disposition 'bad sessions in other respects'.[13] I did not tell mother about these terrible fits of anxiety, and I don't think she ever guessed at them', said Agatha.[14]

In September 1902, Agatha's sister Madge married James Watts, grandson of prosperous Manchester businessman Sir James Watts of Abney Hall, Cheadle, Cheshire. The couple set up home at nearby Cheadle Hall, and each Boxing Day the two families, as was traditional, came together to attend the pantomime in Manchester. The following year Madge and James had a son, James, or 'Jack' as he was known—'a rosy-cheeked, golden-haired little boy... [and] a never-ending source of enjoyment to me', said Agatha.[15]

Meanwhile, back at home in Torquay, roller skating on the pier, at the Assembly Rooms or at the Bath Saloons (where at other times, the important dances were held), were favourite pastimes. However, at the Torquay Regatta it was the accompanying fair, rather than the yacht racing, which attracted Agatha. She also described garden parties where everyone was dressed up 'to the nines'.[16]

During her early childhood, Agatha spent much of her time alone: largely because she was prevented from going to school, and because her siblings, Madge and Monty, were a decade older than herself and were away at boarding school. But by virtue of her creative and imaginative nature she was always able to amuse herself. She later remarked that it puzzled her when children complained that they had 'nothing to do'. Her reply was:

'But you've got a lot of toys, haven't you?'
'Not really.'
'But you've got two trains. And lorries, and a painting set. And blocks. Can't you play with some of them?'
'But I can't play by *myself* with them.'
'Why not?'[17]

However, when Nursie retired, said Agatha, 'I missed her terribly',[18] and 'I was, naturally, at a loss for a playmate',[19] and later, when her French governess, Marie Sijé, returned to France, having been with the family for three years, Agatha did admit to being 'very lonely'.[20]

It is recognized today that a child develops his or her intellectual and inter-personal relationship skills more quickly when in the company of his or her peer group, say in crèches, nursery schools and junior schools rather than in isolation at home, and Agatha was undoubtedly deprived in this respect.

Having learned to read at an early age, Agatha was able to enjoy the collections of fairy tales and other stories given to her by her maternal great aunt Margaret Miller—known as 'Auntie Grannie'. She read these over and over again and co-opted Marie her governess to re-enact various fairy stories with her at performances staged after dinner in front of her parents Clara and Frederick.[21] In fact, drama was to play a large part in Agatha's upbringing, and she described visits to the local theatre in Torquay as one of the great joys of her life.[22]

Time and again in her autobiography, Agatha alluded to the fact that it was her childhood loneliness which was the catalyst which led her to use her imagination to invent imaginary playmates and dramas. For example, she described 'The Kittens', whose names were 'Clover' and 'Blackie', and whose mother's name was 'Mrs Benson'. Later, there was 'Mrs Green' who had a hundred children: the important ones being 'Poodle', 'Squirrel' and 'Tree'. Nursie, for her part possessed a repertoire of six stories, all of which revolved around the various children of the families by whom she had previously been employed. To Agatha, 'Nursie represented the rock of stability in my life....'[23]

By the age of 5, Agatha had created more imaginary characters, including 'Dickie' (based on Goldie the canary) and 'Dicksmistress' (based on herself). On her fifth birthday she was given a dog—a four-month-old Yorkshire terrier puppy which she named 'Toby'. The event, she said, gave her such unimaginable joy that it left her practically speechless.[24] Dogs would play an important part in Agatha's life, and one in particular, not Toby but Peter, would be a source of comfort to her in the troubled times that lay ahead.

Meanwhile, even inanimate objects could be transformed. For example, it was her hoop, said Agatha, which gave her most pleasure in childhood. It could represent to her such objects as a horse, a sea monster, or a railway train, and she imagined herself to be alternately engine driver, guard, or passenger on three railways which were of her own invention.[25] It was the hoop which solved Agatha's problem of being at a loss for company when Nursie retired. She now retreated into her own little world with her hoop as her playmate.[26] Other toys included a rocking horse, a dolls' house and a painted horse and cart—driven by pedals—all of which also doubtless featured in her make-believe adventures. When Agatha grew up and married and subsequently had a daughter of her own—i.e. Rosalind, she could not understand why the child did not enjoy such simple pleasures as she had done in her own childhood.[27]

Had Agatha always intended to be a writer? The answer is no, because, in her youth, her main preoccupation was with music and drama. It was her mother Clara's wish that Agatha learn the pianoforte, which she did under the auspices of Fräulein Uder, a 'formidable little German woman'. She also learnt to dance at Torquay's Athenaeum Rooms; her dancing mistress being Miss Hickey, 'a wonderful, if alarming personality'.[28]

Agatha played the mandolin in a small 'orchestra' which included the five daughters of the family of Dr Huxley—said to be 'by far the most fashionable doctor in Torquay'.[29] This little group, together with some other friends, were also to stage a performance of Gilbert and Sullivan's *The Yeomen of the Guard*. One of the highlights of Agatha's young life was going to the theatre in Exeter to see the famous veteran actor Sir Henry Irving, playing in Alfred Lord Tennyson's tragic drama *Becket*.

Agatha's mother decided, finally, that her daughter, now in her early teens, should have a little 'schooling' at a school for girls in Torquay run by a Miss Guyer. When Agatha returned home from school, however, the same problem of having nobody to play with persisted. She therefore invented yet more imaginary playmates (there being no next-door neighbours with children of her age). She even invented an imaginary school; sketching the characters of the girls and their different social stations, and describing their adventures and the games which they played together.

A year later, Agatha commenced at a finishing school in Paris, run by a Miss Dryden, which she attended for about two months. Particular pleasures for her at this time included going to the opera, and learning dancing, deportment, and drama. She continued with her pianoforte lessons: this time under the auspices of an elderly lady called Madame Legrand, with whom she played duets. Sometimes, because of the zest with which her tutor played and her 'absorption' in the music, she failed to notice that her pupil had lost her place in playing the bass part. The result was, said Agatha, a 'hideous cacophony'.[30]

Agatha took singing lessons, and was soon able to sing many of Schubert's songs in German, and also arias from various famous Italian operas. In particular, she shared her sister Madge's love for the operas of German composer Richard Wagner, and dreamt that she herself might one day sing 'Isolde' in Wagner's music-drama *Tristan and Isolde*. However, she was told that her voice was not strong enough to sing opera.[31] Alternatively, she thought she might become a professional actress. During this period, May, the niece of her American godmother Mrs Sullivan, invited her to Italy to see Florence with its art and architecture.[32]

Agatha described two winters and one summer that she spent in Paris, where, at long last, she could enjoy the company of people her own age, as amongst the happiest days she had ever known. In 1910, she returned home from Paris, by which time her mother was seriously ill. When the doctors who attended her made a variety of diagnoses, none of which were correct, Clara said, 'I don't think they *know*. I don't know myself. I think the great thing is to get out of the doctors' hands.' She then proposed to Agatha that they let the house and go to Egypt for the winter.

For Agatha, the creative instinct to write was present from an early age. After all, as an avid reader herself, and one who enjoyed being read to, it is hardly surprising that she herself was moved to put pen to paper. The first story which she wrote as a child, she described as a 'melodrama' concerning two noble ladies and a castle. She showed it to her sister Madge, who proposed that they should perform it as a play.

Agatha described her first attempts at poetry as being 'unbelievably awful'. However, she persevered, and duly appeared in print at the age of 11, with a poem about the first trams (electrically powered omnibuses running on rails) which came to Ealing (home of her maternal great-aunt Margaret Miller). By her late teens she had won several prizes and some of her poems were printed in *The Poetry Review*.[33] She declared, however, that her only ambition for the future was to have 'a happy marriage'.[34]

Agatha was lying in bed one day, convalescing and feeling bored after an attack of influenza, when her mother suggested that she attempt another story. The result was *The House of Beauty*. Several others followed, all typed by her on her sister Madge's 'Empire' typewriter. These were offered to various magazines, but to no avail.

She then attempted to write a novel, set in Cairo and based on three characters which she had encountered in the dining room of the hotel where she and her mother had stayed. In that city, said Agatha, she attended five dances each week. She was then just seventeen years old. At that time in her life she admitted to having little interest in 'the wonders of antiquity', and for this reason declined to accompany her mother on a journey up the Nile to Luxor and Karnak. However, some twenty years later, 'the beauties of Egypt' were to impress her mightily, as will be seen. Although she was, in her own words, having far too good a time to fall in love with anyone, Agatha revealed that she did receive at least two proposals of matrimony during this time![35]

Agatha entitled her novel *Snow Upon the Desert*. When her mother Clara, asked a neighbour, the novelist Eden Philpotts, to advise as to the next step, he put Agatha in contact with his own literary agent Hugh Massie. Although Massie declined to accept this particular work, he encouraged Agatha by suggesting that she commence work on another.[36]

When Agatha said that she would like to try her hand at writing a detective story, her sister Madge's response was as follows. She had given it some thought, and decided that the project was too difficult a one for Agatha to undertake. This was seen not only as a challenge; it also triggered an obstinate streak in the younger sister. From that time onwards, Agatha 'was fired by the determination' to write a detective story![37]

Although Agatha's mother had denied her daughter a formal schooling until she was in her early teens, nevertheless it has to be said that it was Clara, along with her elder sister Madge, who were the main catalysts as far as Agatha's creative writing was concerned.

CHAPTER 11

Romance, War, Serious Writing, Marriage

In her youth, Agatha had several suitors before she finally met her husband-to-be; one of whom was Reggie Lucy, a major in the Gunners, who helped to teach her the game of golf, and to whom she became engaged.[1]

It was Agatha's opinion that the position of women, over the years, had not changed for the better, largely because they had 'behaved like mugs'. They had demanded to be allowed to do the same work as men, who in their turn had embraced the idea all too readily—after all, why should a man work to support a wife, when that wife was perfectly able to support herself? If this is what she wanted, then so be it! As far as Agatha was concerned, the sad thing was that women, having successfully portrayed themselves as the 'weaker sex', would now be roughly on the same level as those women of primitive tribes, who were obliged to labour all day in the fields. Agatha envied the women of Victorian times who, in her view, were in a much better position. In those days, women were seen as being frail, delicate, and in constant need of being 'protected and cherished'. In return for these favours, the woman accepted that the man was head of the household. When a woman married, she, for her part, accepted the man's role in the world, and his way of life. These concepts appeared to Agatha to be sensible and 'the foundation of happiness'.[2]

But Agatha also believed that there was more to marriage than the couple simply being lovers. She took the old-fashioned view that *respect* was essential. The wife wished to feel that her husband was someone of integrity, someone on whom she could rely, and a person of sound judgment. He must be trustworthy, and reliable enough to make difficult decisions, as and when they needed to be made.[3]

Agatha first met her husband-to-be Archie Christie, at a dance given by the Cliffords of Chudleigh, Devonshire, to which members of the local army garrison from Exeter were invited. It was 12 October 1912. She was aged 22, and he 23. From then on, the couple enjoyed going to dances and attending concerts together. Archie, an army officer, was currently awaiting admission to the newly-created Royal Flying Corps, and would soon commence training on Salisbury Plain. He told Agatha that this would be the 'the service of the future', and that if ever war was to break out again then aeroplanes would be the first things that would be required.[4] However, when Archie made Agatha a proposal of marriage, she declined, pointing out that she was already engaged (to Reggie Lucy). However, he persisted, and in the end she relented.

Agatha described, in somewhat rueful terms, Archie's letters to her at that time. Instead of being romantic, as she had hoped, they were 'full of technical accounts of Farman biplanes and Avros'. Nevertheless, to be involved with this new form of transportation—flying—was 'glamorous', she said, and of Archie she was immensely proud.[5] As for Agatha's mother Clara, she had reservations about Archie, whom she described as 'ruthless'.[6] Sadly for Agatha, in this respect she proved to be correct.

Early in 1914, Agatha passed her examination in First Aid and Home Nursing. This had involved spending two mornings per week at the local hospital's Out-Patients' Department in Torquay, and also spending a day with the District Nurse. She then joined the Voluntary Aid Detachment (VAD), an organization which provided volunteer nurses for the war effort.

Following the outbreak of war on 4 August 1914, the first casualties began arriving at Torquay railway station, to be taken to an improvised 'hospital'—the converted Town Hall—where Agatha worked as a nursing auxiliary. With accommodation for over 200 patients, it was staffed by a matron, eight trained nurses, and VADs like Agatha. She enjoyed nursing and said, that, had she not married, she would have 'trained as a real hospital nurse'.[7] On 5 August her fiancé Archie left for France with the British Expeditionary Force.

Meanwhile, Agatha's brother Monty rejoined the Army—the King's African Rifles—which would see action in German East Africa. Prior to this, said Agatha, her brother:

had not featured largely in any of our lives....[8] In every family there is usually one member who is a source of trouble and worry. My brother Monty was ours. Until the day of his death [in 1929] he was always causing someone a headache.[9]

Monty was subsequently wounded in the arm. The wound became infected, and when he was discharged from the Army he returned to England, bringing his African servant Shebani with him. Having been successfully treated for his infection in London, Monty and his servant moved to Ashfield, the Millers' family home in Torquay, and subsequently to a small bungalow on Dartmoor.

Agatha duly married Archibald—'Archie'—Christie on Christmas Eve 1914 at the Parish Church of Emmanuel, Clifton, Bristol.[10] Archie was currently serving in France as an aviator in the Royal Flying Corps. The couple had their honeymoon at Torquay's Grand Hotel, and spent Christmas Day with Agatha's mother. On Boxing Day, Agatha travelled with Archie to London and said goodbye to him as he left, once more, for France. She would not see him for another six months.

In the summer of 1915, Agatha met Archie in London as he had three days of leave. It was now that Archie's days of active flying came to an end, owing to a sinus condition.[11] It was not until October 1915 that the couple were to meet again; this time for a short break in Hampshire's New Forest. Three further periods of leave followed, but not until 1917.

Meanwhile, late in 1915, Agatha commenced work at Torquay Hospital's dispensary, where she studied for the Apothecaries Hall Examination and was tutored by one of Torquay's leading commercial pharmacists. 'Naturally, when one is a novice at this kind of job, one has a nervous horror of making mistakes,' she said. Although there was always another dispenser to check when a poison was added to a medicine, there could still be 'frightening moments', when a mistake could be made.[12] (The word 'poison' had different connotations in the early twentieth century to that which it has today. Then, pharmacists were governed by the Poisons and Pharmacy Act of 1908, where virtually all substances which would now be called 'medicines' were classed as 'poisons'.) Agatha, subsequently, composed a poem entitled *In a Dispensary*, featuring real poisons such as 'Monkshood Blue', 'Aconite', and 'Deadly Cyanide'.

It was while she was working in the dispensary, said Agatha, that the idea of writing a detective story began to crystallise in her mind. 'Since I was surrounded by poisons, perhaps it was natural that death by poisoning should be the method I selected.'[13] In the course of her future life as a writer of detective fiction, a knowledge of 'poisons' would prove to be invaluable!

As for her detective, Agatha was determined that he should be quite different from others (such as Sir Arthur Conan Doyle's Sherlock Holmes). She therefore, decided to make him a Belgian: there being a number of Belgian war refugees living in her local parish of Tor. A retired Chief of the Belgian Police Force, he would be tidy in his habits and very brainy[14]—the phrase the 'little grey cells of the mind' appealing to her in this regard. Finally, she settled on his name: 'Hercule Poirot'.

Having written the first draft of her book in longhand, and transcribed it, using the old typewriter that had once belonged to her sister Madge, she found that the intricacies of the plot were getting the better of her. Her mother then proposed that she go away for a holiday, in order to concentrate. The outcome was that Agatha spent a fortnight at the Moorland Hotel at Hay Tor on Dartmoor, where she completed her book which she called *The Mysterious Affair at Styles*, a murder mystery in which the victim was poisoned by strychnine! However, the publisher (Hodder & Stoughton), to whom she sent the volume, returned it. When she received a similar rejection from another publisher, Methuen, she sent it to a third, viz. the Bodley Head, who promptly 'forgot all about it'. In the event, the Bodley Head kept Agatha's manuscript for almost two years before finally agreeing to publish, and then only after considerable changes were made.[15]

The First World War ended on 11 November 1918, by which time Archie had reached the rank of colonel, at the young age of 29. During the war he had displayed conspicuous bravery: being mentioned four times in Dispatches and decorated with the CMG, the DSO, and the Star of the Order of St Stanislaus, Third Class (by the Russian Empire).[16] He was now employed by the Air Ministry in London, where the couple set up home. On 5 August 1919 their daughter Rosalind was born.

CHAPTER 12

Terrifying Dreams: The 'Gun Man'

To the outsider, Agatha, as a child, led a seemingly idyllic existence. She lived in a beautiful place on the coast of the 'English Riviera'; loved both her parents as they loved her, and, although lacking friends of her own age, was able to compensate for this by creating friends in her imagination. However, in every Garden of Eden there is a serpent, which in her case took the form of terrifying dreams.

For centuries, people have attempted to analyse dreams—the meaning of which can sometimes appear obvious, and at other times obscure. Agatha's dreams are instructive, in that they shed light on her mental state as a child. They indicate that, surprising as it may seem, she was a person who, by her own admission, suffered from deep feelings of anxiety and insecurity. And these feelings would one day manifest themselves once again, as already indicated, when the great crisis in her life came to a head in December 1926.

In attempting to understand Agatha's bad dreams, it is first necessary to describe them. According to her, they centred around someone whom she called 'The Gun Man' (or 'Gunman'). She had given him this appellation because he carried a gun—obviously—but she was not frightened that he would shoot her. The gun, described as 'an old-fashioned type of musket', was simply an appendage of someone who otherwise appeared to her as a Frenchman 'in grey-blue uniform, powdered hair in a cue [pigtail or plait], and a kind of three-cornered hat'. No, it was the mere presence of the Frenchman that frightened her, together with the fact that he would appear during the course of a very ordinary dream, say when she was at a tea party, or walking with family or friends, or attending a festive event. Suddenly, she would be overcome with a feeling of uneasiness, knowing that there was someone present '*who ought not to be there*'. This feeling quickly gave way to 'a horrid feeling of fear', when she would suddenly see The Gunman, either sitting at the tea table, walking along a beach, or joining in with some party games. 'His pale-blue eyes would meet mine, and I would wake up shrieking, 'The Gunman, The Gunman!'

There were, however, variations to the dream, in that The Gunman, instead of being a separate entity in himself, sometimes masqueraded as another person. For example, Agatha would be sitting at the tea table when she would look across to one of her relations, or to a friend, and realize that it was not her aunt, her brother, or her mother whom she was looking at. Instead, as she looked at the familiar face with its characteristically pale-blue eyes, she would suddenly realize '*It was really the Gunman*'.[1] Agatha herself had no idea what the origin of these dreams was. Could The Gunman have emanated from a story that she had read? No, she had never read anything about anyone who remotely resembled him!

In her autobiography, Agatha gave the impression that her 'nightmares', as she described them, were at their most frequent when she was about four years old,[2] and she makes no mention of them occurring in her teenage or adult years (even though certain traumatic events which occurred subsequently were to remind her of them and of The Gunman).

Experts in the field of sleep disorders differentiate between 'Nightmare Disorder' and 'Sleep Terror Disorder' (or 'Night Terrors').

> The essential feature of Nightmare Disorder is the repeated occurrence of frightening dreams that lead to awakenings from sleep.

Such dreams, which may 'cause the individual significant distress', are most likely to occur late in the night. Their onset is often between the ages of three and six years, and most children 'outgrow' the problem.[3] On the other hand:

> The essential feature of Sleep Terror Disorder is the repeated occurrence of sleep terrors, that is, abrupt awakenings from sleep usually beginning with a panicky scream or cry.

Sleep terrors usually begin during the first part of the night.

> During an episode, the individual is difficult to awaken or comfort. During a typical episode, the individual abruptly sits up in bed screaming or crying, with a frightened expression.... Sleep Terror Disorder usually begins in children aged between four and twelve years and resolves spontaneously during adolescence.[4]

Agatha's words, 'I would wake up shrieking...' therefore indicate that it was 'Night Terrors', from which she suffered as a child (and which an estimated five per cent of children experience).

Dr John Bowlby made a study, highlighting the importance of the 'attachment' which occurs between the young child and its family, and in particular its parents ('attachment' being defined by him as, 'a reciprocal system of behaviours between an infant and a caregiver—generally the mother'). Said he:

> It seems likely that early attachment to one, or a few close relatives holds portent for a person's overall relational ability. Attachment predicts the ability to relate to many others; to establish trust, to form and retain friendships, and to engage in mutually satisfying emotional and physical relationships.[5]

Of the mutual love and affection that existed between Agatha and her parents there is no doubt, and more than once she stated that her own principal ambition was to reproduce this idyllic environment by achieving a happy marriage herself.

Conversely, Bowlby describes a condition called 'separation anxiety', which:

> is usually caused by adverse family experiences, such as repeated threats of abandonment or rejections by parents, or to parents' or siblings' illnesses or deaths, for which the child feels responsible.[6]

Clearly, Agatha's parents had absolutely no intention of abandoning their daughter. Quite the opposite in fact, for by keeping Agatha from attending school, Clara made it inevitable that she and other members of the family were in close proximity to one another for longer periods than would otherwise have been the case. And even when Agatha did eventually go to school, it was only for two days a week.[7] When Clara and Frederick decided to spend the winter on the Continent, and when Clara went to Cairo to convalesce after an illness, Agatha accompanied them. And when Clara sent Agatha to Paris to continue her schooling there, Clara went with her.

However, there were several reasons why Agatha, as a child, might have felt insecure and afraid. For example, she may have wondered whether, like her two siblings, she would be sent away to boarding school.

As already mentioned, Agatha's family placed its reliance for the future on income to be provided by the investments from her grandfather Nathaniel Miller's will; but because these investments had been unwisely made, this income did not materialise.[8] Despite this setback, Frederick persistently refused to contemplate seeking any form of gainful employment for himself, and the resultant financial insecurity caused his wife, Clara, much anxiety throughout Agatha's childhood, and led her to have grave forebodings about the future. The subject of 'ruin' featured often in the many novels that Agatha had read, where the victim would threaten to blow out his brains, and the heroine be forced to vacate her sumptuous mansion and live thereafter in rags and penury.[9] Believing passionately, on the one hand, that her father Frederick, was 'the rock upon which the home is set',[10] and seeing the well-being of his household being jeopardized because of his inertia on the other, must have created an unsettling confusion and consequent insecurity in Agatha's mind which she would have found difficult to resolve.

Neither of her parents enjoyed good health, and were she to lose one, or worse still both of them, this would also be a true catastrophe.

Agatha's parents, and especially her father Frederick, caused her anxiety in another respect, in that neither of them appeared to take their Christian faith as seriously as she thought they should. Said she:

> I had terrible fears for the ultimate salvation of my father, who played croquet blithely on Sunday afternoons [i.e. the Sabbath Day] and made gay jokes about curates and, even, once, about a bishop.[11]

And of course, for the 'sinner', there was always the prospect of going to 'hell'. This is reflected in Agatha's novel *Unfinished Portrait*, where Celia, the heroine, is described as a 'serious little girl' who gave God much thought, and whose desire was to be 'good and holy'. Hell, according to Celia, was where people went if they were 'wicked'. She, however, was confident, that rather than going to hell and burning in 'hell-fire', she would go to heaven because she would always be good. However, she was desperately anxious for Daddy to go to heaven[12] (and, of course, Mummy also).

Could it therefore be the case, that such fears as have been described above were the source of Agatha's nightmares—as she described them—featuring The Gun Man?

In her autobiography, Agatha's first mention of her 'Gun Man' dreams comes when she is aged four. Was it pure coincidence that, immediately prior to this, she had described an episode when she left the immediate and safe confines of her home to go primrose-picking with Nursie? Suddenly, this idyllic scene of rural tranquillity was shattered. A 'giant of a man, angry and red-faced', who from the way he spoke was probably a gamekeeper, appeared from nowhere and accused the pair of trespassing. What was far worse, he threatened Agatha with a horrific death—that of being boiled alive. Although Agatha made no mention of the man carrying a gun, and declared that, 'in nightmares, I never relived this particular experience', nevertheless, it remains a possibility that in her subconscious mind, the alleged gamekeeper became The Gunman of her nightmares.[13]

One may imagine Agatha, as a young child, retiring to bed and playing a little game in her mind with her imaginary playmates before drifting off to sleep. She dreams that she is in a familiar setting, in the bosom of her family and friends, and all is well. Then, suddenly, The Gunman appears, threatening to disrupt this happy, tranquil scene, by supplanting one or other of those whom she holds most dear, be they male or female, but in particular her mother Clara, with himself. She wakes up, screaming in terror.

When Agatha's father Frederick died, one of her worst fears was realised, as is indicated by her in *Unfinished Portrait*, where Frederick is personified by 'John'. When John dies, Celia his daughter is dumbfounded. She finds herself in the garden, wandering about, trying to come to terms with the loss. For the moment, her world had collapsed. Although everything still looked the same—the ash tree, the path—it was somehow different. 'It was like the Gun Man—everything all right and then *he* was there…'. She was now forced to accept the fact that '*Things could change—things could happen…*'. She wondered if her father was now in heaven, and if so, whether he was happy. 'Oh, Daddy… She began to cry.'[14]

The subject of dreams has fascinated people from time immemorial, and their interpretation has taxed the brains of the world's greatest psychiatrists, psychologists and thinkers; not least the great Sigmund Freud himself. As for their origins and meanings, even to those with a medical background, attempting to decipher a mass of psychiatrist's terminology and make sense of, often, contradictory analyses by different persons of the same dream, is a daunting prospect—but nevertheless a fascinating one.

The words of psychologist Calvin S. Hall, who has made a study of dreams and their causation, lends weight to the notion that 'strangers', such as, in this instance, The Gun Man, 'represent the unknown, the ambiguous, and the uncertain'.[15] As for Agatha, it is difficult to escape the conclusion that, as a deeply insecure and anxious child, she was particularly vulnerable to night terrors. The fear of change, of losing her home, but more importantly of being separated from her loved ones, was a cardinal feature of Agatha's make up; a fact which was to have far-reaching consequences for her future well-being, as will be seen later when the Gun Man reappeared, and the idyllic world for which she had always longed was shattered beyond recognition.

CHAPTER 13

Married Life with Archie

In 1924 the Christie family moved to 'Scotswood', a large Victorian house in Sunningdale, Berkshire. It had been divided into flats, one of which the couple decided to rent. Said Agatha:

> We were all terribly pleased to get to Scotswood; it was so exciting to be in the country again: Archie was delighted, because he was now in close proximity to Sunningdale Golf Course. Site [Miss White, who served as 'mother's help'] was pleased because she was saved the long treks to the park, and Rosalind because she had the garden for her Fairy cycle [a bicycle manufactured by the Colson Company of Ohio, USA, and marketed under the name 'Fairy']. So everyone was happy.[1]

However, because of Archie's preoccupation with golf, 'our weekends now were the dullest time for me'.[2]

> It was by now just beginning to dawn on me that perhaps I *might* be a writer by profession. I was not sure of it yet. I still had an idea that writing books was only the natural successor to embroidering sofa-cushions.[3]

Agatha now decided to employ 'a combined secretary and governess', and the outcome was that Miss Charlotte Fisher:

> tall, brown-haired, about twenty three, I judged; had had experience with children, looked extremely capable, and had a nice-looking twinkle behind her general decorum

was appointed to the post.[4] 'Carlo', as Rosalind nicknamed her, had a sister Mary, who lived in London and was also willing to help Agatha out in times of need.[5]

> 'We could afford another baby now,' I pointed out. I had been contemplating this for some time with a good deal of pleasure.
> Archie waved aside another baby. 'I don't want anyone but Rosalind,' he said. 'Rosalind is absolutely satisfactory, quite enough.'
> Archie was mad about Rosalind. He enjoyed playing with her, and she even cleaned his golf clubs. They understood each other, I think, better than Rosalind and I did. They had the same sense of humour, and saw each other's point of view.[6]

Here, Agatha is regretting the fact that Rosalind had not bonded with her in the same way that her daughter had bonded with Archie. In early 1926 the Christies moved to a house of their own: Styles, also in Sunningdale.

Archie was in Spain when Agatha's mother Clara died on 5 April 1926, following a severe attack of bronchitis,[7] and he was therefore unable to attend the funeral. When it came to 'the problem of clearing up Ashfield', Agatha's beloved family home at Torquay, Archie declined to help, owing to the expense of the journey, and also because, as 'he could not get off before Saturday and would have to go back Sunday night, it would hardly be worth it'.[8] As for Agatha's sister Madge, she was 'too embroiled in her own concerns'.[9] Finally, to make matters worse, Carlo was obliged to travel to Edinburgh to look after her sick father. 'A terrible sense of loneliness was coming over me,' said Agatha.[10] And when Archie did eventually join her at Ashfield, she regarded him as *'a stranger'*.

> He went through the motions of ordinary greetings, but he was, quite simply, not Archie. I did not know what was the matter with him.[11]

When Agatha confronted her husband, he told her that he had fallen in love and would like her to give him a divorce 'as soon as it can be arranged'. Said she:

> I suppose, with those words, that part of my life—my happy, successful confident life—ended.[12] I thought he would get over it. But he didn't. He left Sunningdale. Carlo had come back to me by then ... and it was a terrific comfort to have her there.[13]
>
> What I could not understand was his continued unkindness to me during that period. He would hardly speak to me or answer when he was spoken to. Because his conscience troubled him he could not help behaving with a certain ruthlessness. So, after illness [i.e. depression], came sorrow, despair and heartbreak. There is no need to dwell on it. I stood out for a year, hoping he would change. But he did not. So ended my first married life.[14]

On 23 January 1927, the month after her disappearance, Agatha, Carlo and Rosalind set sail from Southampton aboard the line *Geiria*, for a holiday in the Canary Islands.[15] This conflicts with the statement which Agatha made in her autobiography—that she went to the Canary Islands in February.[16] On her return she rented a flat in Chelsea, near to the home of Madge's sister-in-law Nan Kon.[17] Subsequently, following a meeting between Agatha and Archie, when he told her 'there's only one thing that I really want. I want madly to be happy, and I can't be happy unless I can get married to Nancy,'[18] divorce proceedings were put in train.

* * *

Therefore, yes, Agatha's autobiography does provide certain clues as to her state of mind in December 1926. For example, she had recently lost her beloved mother. She was unhappy and lonely in her marriage, particularly when Archie was playing golf. She would have liked to have had another baby, but her husband refused to contemplate it. She was saddened by the fact that Rosalind had failed to bond with her as she had bonded with Archie. She felt that he ought to have made the effort to help her clear up Ashfield, following the death of her mother. Also, she described Archie as being unkind. Finally, Archie had an affair and asked Agatha for a divorce. He had now become 'a stranger to her'.

Although Agatha, in her autobiography, describes the tensions that were apparent in her marriage to Archie, it was in a novel, published under a pseudonym, that the most important clues were to be found. In it, Agatha was to shed further light on her true feelings over this period, for the heroine of the story, 'Celia', is, in almost every respect, Agatha in disguise.

CHAPTER 14

Unfinished Portrait
(The author's comments are in italics)

Agatha Christie's novel *Unfinished Portrait*, was published in 1934 under the pseudonym Mary Westmacott. Both the story and the characters depicted therein contain many parallels with Agatha's own life.

Celia, the heroine, encountered Larraby, a portrait painter, whilst on holiday on an island.[1] At the time, Celia was contemplating suicide, her mother Miriam having died and her marriage having ended in divorce.

For 'Miriam' read Clara, for 'Dermot', Archie, for 'Judy', Rosalind, and for 'Cyril', Monty.

Describing her suicidal thoughts, Celia declared:

> I've thought about it a good deal … and it really is best. It's simple and easy and quick. And it won't be inconvenient to anybody.[2]

Larraby enquired of Celia if she had been happy as a child.

> 'Oh, *yes!*' There was no doubting the eager certainty of her assent. She went on: 'Too happy.'
>   'Is that possible?'
>   'I think so. You see, you're not prepared for the things that happen. You never conceive that they might happen.'[3]

When Larraby told her that he too had:

> 'stood where you are now—I've felt as you feel that life isn't worth living. I've known that blinding despair that can only see one way out.'

she answered by alluding to the fact that she had once attempted suicide. 'I had one try—that didn't come off. And afterwards I was glad that it hadn't.'[4]

This implied that Agatha herself had once attempted suicide—witness, her alleged attempt to drive over the edge of the chalk pit at Newlands Corner.

Celia now revealed that she was aged 39.

Agatha herself was aged 36 when she made her attempt at suicide.

Following her divorce, Celia told Larraby, 'I simply can't face it, that's all. Another thirty-five long empty years.'[5]

'Do you believe in an afterwards?' [i.e. an afterlife], Larraby enquired of Celia, to which the latter replied regretfully:

'I'm afraid,' she said slowly, 'I do. Just nothing would be almost too good to be true. Just going to sleep—peacefully—and just not waking up. That *would* be so lovely.'[6]

Celia remembered her childhood, when her brother Cyril 'went away', and she 'was left with her mother', and 'had her mother all to herself'.[7]

In real life, Agatha's brother Monty, went to South Africa in 1899 to fight in the South African War.
Celia 'adored her mother's stories'.[8]

Likewise Agatha, who stated that her mother Clara had no need to refer to a book because she carried all her stories in her head.
Celia found Miriam to be a source of great comfort.

If she woke up with a scream after dreaming of the Gun Man, she would jump out of bed, knowing her way perfectly in the dark, and run along the passage to her mother's room. And her mother would come back with her and sit for a while, saying, 'There is no Gun Man, darling. You're quite safe—you're quite safe.' And then Celia would fall asleep again, knowing that Mummy had indeed made everything safe ...[9]

This is reminiscent of Agatha as a child, after a bad dream featuring the 'Gun Man', being comforted by her mother Clara, whom she mentions in her autobiography as playing exactly the same role as Miriam.

Miriam had theories of her own as to education. She was a good teacher, clear in explanation, and able to arouse enthusiasm over any subject she selected.
She had a passion for history, and under her guidance Celia was swept from one event to another in the world's life story.[10]

However, said Larraby, insightfully of Celia, 'She inherited something from Miriam—a dangerous intensity of affection.'[11]

As her piano playing improved she would spend long hours in the big schoolroom [of her house], turning out old dusty piles of music and reading them. Old songs—'Down the Vale', 'A Song of Sleep', 'Fiddle and I'. She would sing them, her voice rising clear and pure. She was rather vain about her voice.[12]

Agatha too loved music, playing the pianoforte and singing.

Celia ... spent much of her time alone.[13]

So did Agatha, in her childhood.

When Celia and her family were holidaying in France, Jeanne, an apprentice dressmaker, 'was very astonished when the English lady [Miriam] spoke to her and asked whether she would like to come to England',[14] which she did. However, Jeanne subsequently became homesick, and finally returned to her native land.[15]

Agatha's French teacher/governess/nurse/companion was Marie Sijé, from Pau in southern France, whom the Christies had encountered in similar circumstances.

Miriam told Celia it was time for her to go to Paris. It had always been understood that Celia was to be 'finished' in Paris. There, she would study singing, piano playing, drawing and painting, and French.[16]

Agatha, too, attended finishing school in Paris.

Said Larraby,

Cyril went into the Army and had gone abroad to India before Celia came out! [i.e. was introduced to society at the age of seventeen or eighteen, usually at a ball] He never loomed very large in her life—or in Miriam's.[17]

However, on one occasion when Cyril was at home, 'he was gruff and uncomfortable'.[18]

An allusion to Agatha's distant relationship with her brother Monty.

Grannie lived at Wimbledon, and Celia liked staying with her very much.[19]

A parallel with 'Auntie Grannie'—Agatha's maternal great-aunt Margaret Miller, with whom she stayed as a child, and who lived in Ealing.

Celia's father died when she was ten years old. Momentarily her world was shattered.[20]

Agatha's father Frederick Miller, died in November 1901, a painful and traumatic event for the 11-year-old child.

Dermot was a soldier[21] with 'a decided manner, an air of being able to get his own way always—under any circumstances'.[22] He was aged 23 when he asked Celia to marry him.[23]

Archie, also a military men, was also aged 23 when he became engaged to Agatha.

In the early stages of Celia's relationship with Dermot, Miriam declared, 'That young man—I don't like him.'[24] But when Celia challenged her mother about this, she replied ambiguously, 'I do like him. I think he's very attractive—very attractive indeed. But not considerate.'[25]

Miriam told herself that she had been unduly suspicious and hostile towards the man who had taken her daughter away from her.[26]

Clara had a similar change of heart in regard to Archie, and mellowed in her attitude towards him.

However, Celia's grannie advised her to 'Remember, dear, men are not to be trusted.'[27]

In the year of Celia's engagement to Dermot, war broke out.[28] 'A Red Cross hospital was being opened near Celia's home, but she must pass her First Aid and Nursing exams.'[29] However, 'Celia never took up Red Cross work.'[30]

In contrast, Agatha worked for almost the entire duration of the war: first as a VAD nurse, and subsequently in Torquay Hospital's Dispensary.

Dermot got wounded in the arm and came home to a hospital. On his recovery he was passed fit for home service and was sent to the War Office. He and Celia were married.[31] For Celia, marriage ... was the 'living happily ever afterwards' of her favourite fairy tales.[32]

In fact, it was Monty who was wounded in the arm. (He died in the autumn of 1929 from a cerebral haemorrhage.)[33] *Archie's complaint was sinusitis, which obliged him to cut short his flying career. He subsequently worked for the Air Ministry.*

    As for Celia

She had been, half-consciously, a little afraid of Dermot.

This begs the question, was Agatha equally afraid of Archie?

He had been a stranger to her. She had felt that though she loved him she knew nothing about him. Their aims, their minds, their characters were poles apart …[34]

On learning of her engagement to Dermot, Cyril, 'who was fighting in Mesopotamia', wrote a letter of disapproval to Celia.[35]

Monty may have disapproved of Archie, just as, according to Agatha, he disapproved of almost everybody else!

The couple commenced their married life in London, where Celia was lonely. She would have liked to have taken up 'hospital work' but Dermot 'negatived the idea violently'. However, he did permit her to embark upon a course of typewriting, shorthand, and book-keeping.[36]

Dermot was not demonstrative. He never said, 'I love you', hardly ever attempted a spontaneous caress.[37] Talking about thoughts and feelings seemed to him a waste of time. He liked realities—not ideas.[38] He disliked being touched, or leaned on for comfort, or asked to enter into other people's emotion. So Celia fought heroically against her passion for sharing, her weakness for caresses, her longing her reassurance.[39]

On learning that Celia was expecting a baby, 'Dermot was terribly upset', fearing that she would 'think of it all the time and not of me'.[40] When Judy duly arrived, Celia employed a nurse, Kate, to look after her.

    Following the Armistice which ended hostilities in the First World War, Dermot decided that 'as soon as possible he would get demobilised and would go into the City. He knew of an opening in a very good firm'.[41]

Archie too, found employment in the City.

    In their early married life, the couple enjoyed weekend walks together in the countryside.[42] However, when Dermot took up golf and joined a golf club, even this pleasure was denied to Celia.[43]

Agatha declared that weekends were her most lonely time, for that selfsame reason.

However, Dermot was encouraging when she suggested that she might write a book.[44]

Celia realized that Judy was quite a different character from herself. She 'didn't want to have stories told to her …, wasn't any good at make-believe', and was 'full of common sense. And common sense, Celia found, can be often very depressing'. In fact, 'Judy was a complete puzzle to her mother'.[45] By contrast:

Dermot and Judy had suddenly become friends. A thoroughly satisfying communion had grown up between them. Only when she was ill did she prefer her mother to her father.[46]

A reflection of Agatha and Rosalind's inability to bond with one other.

However, when she was with her own mother Miriam:

Celia loved the feeling of stepping back into her old life. To feel that happy tide of reassurance sweeping over her—the feeling of being loved—of being *adequate*.[47]

When Dermot's firm went into liquidation, and he became unemployed, he was miserable. However, he found another job and became prosperous, whereupon, 'The first thing they bought was a second-hand car.'[48]

Archie's motor car was a Delage. Agatha's was a Morris Cowley.

They then moved into 'the lodge of a big estate' near Dalton Heath, which was ten miles from Dalton Heath golf course. 'They also bought a dog—an adorable sealyham called Aubrey.'[49]

Agatha too, loved her pet dogs.

Celia contacted a publisher who told her that she was 'a born storyteller'. A year later, her first novel was published. 'It was called *Lonely Harbour*.'[50]

Agatha's first novel The Mysterious Affair at Styles, *was published in 1920.*

'Miriam died when Judy was eight years old.' Celia and Dermot were abroad when she had become ill. Celia therefore returned home, but she persuaded Dermot 'to stay behind and finish his holiday'.[51]

When Agatha's mother Clara died in April 1926, her granddaughter Rosalind, was aged six.

Celia thought: 'I'm alone now … Dermot and Judy were strangers [to her] … She thought: 'There's no one to go to any more … Panic swept over her … and then remorse …'[52]

When Celia went to the family home to 'turn out' her late mother's belongings:

a great wave of loneliness passed over her. She felt afraid … How cold the world was … without her mother.[53]

Agatha had depended on her mother for emotional love and support. She was now faced with having to return alone to Ashfield, to sort out Clara's estate.

Celia thought: 'I want to run away …'[54] Celia felt ill. The loneliness of the house was getting on her nerves. She wished she had someone to speak to. There were Judy and Miss Hood, but they belonged to such an alien world that being with them brought more strain than relief.

Even the presence of Rosalind and Carlo could not assuage Agatha's grief.

It was after Judy had gone to bed that the silence of the house wrapped itself round Celia like a pall. It seemed so empty—so empty … She wrote to Dermot and begged him to come down for the weekend.[55]

This is presumably how Agatha felt at Styles, on the evening of Friday 3 December 1926. Archie was with his mistress, Carlo was in London; and Rosalind was in bed asleep.

Celia consulted her doctor who told her that she was 'heading for a breakdown [but] once you get away with your husband into fresh surroundings you'll be as right as rain'.[56] Alas, it was not to be, for when Dermot did finally return home, 'it wasn't Dermot. It was a stranger who looked at her—quick sideways glances—and looked away again …'.[57]

Dermot now announced to Celia that he had fallen in love with Marjorie Connell.

A parallel with Archie's affair with Nancy Neele.

Whereupon, Celia reminded her husband that he and she had been married for eleven years, and that 'it was on this night, nine years ago, that Judy began to be born.[58] How could he—how could he—be so cruel to *me*?' she asked herself.[59]

In her autobiography, Agatha stated that 'Rosalind's birthday was on 5 August [1919]. Archie arrived [from London] on the 3rd'. Very shortly afterwards came the bombshell. Archie asked Agatha for a divorce.[60] She refused to give her consent.

On the day following Judy's birthday, Dermot left.[61]

Celia felt terribly ill. Her legs ached, her head swam. She felt like an old, old woman. The pain in her head increased until she could have screamed.[62]

She finally returned home to The Lodge, where she met with Dermot who enquired, 'How soon can I get my freedom?', by which he meant a divorce.[63] This, Celia refused to countenance.[64]

If he had appealed to Celia, if he had thrown himself on her mercy, if he had told her that he loved Marjorie and wanted her and couldn't live without her, Celia would have melted and agreed to anything he wanted.

But Dermot took an entirely different line. He claimed what he wanted as a right, and tried to bully her into consenting. She had always been so soft, so malleable, that he was astonished at her resistance. She ate practically nothing; she did not sleep; her legs felt so weak she would [i.e. could] hardly walk; she suffered tortures from neuralgia and earache, but she stood firm.

He told her that she was behaving disgracefully, that she was a vulgar, clutching woman, that she ought to be ashamed of herself, that he was ashamed of her. It had no effect.

She grew worried about her physical condition. Sometimes she lost the thread of what she was saying—her thoughts even became confused…

She would wake up in the night in a condition of utter terror. She would feel sure that Dermot was poisoning her—to get her out of the way.[65]

Agatha's novel *The Cornish Mystery*, published in 1923, contained a similar theme. Mrs Pengelly appeals to Poirot for help, in the belief that her husband was trying to poison her!

Is it conceivable that Agatha felt the same way about Archie, and if so, was there any basis for her fears, or did they reflect a certain paranoia on her part—paranoia being defined as 'a pattern of pervasive distrust and suspiciousness of others such that their motives are interpreted as malevolent'?[66] As for Celia:

1 Jack Best, at the place where Agatha's car was found abandoned. *Photo:* Daily Mirror, *courtesy Robert Bartlett*

2 A 1926 Morris Cowley Tourer. *Photo: Malcolm McKay*

3 A 1926 Morris Cowley Tourer showing spare two-gallon petrol tank. *Photo: Malcolm McKay*

4 The Morris Cowley from driver's perspective. *Photo: Malcolm McKay*

5 The Morris Cowley, dashboard in close up. *Photo: Malcolm McKay*

6 The search: Superintendent William Kenward (left). *Photo*: Daily Mail, *courtesy Robert Bartlett*

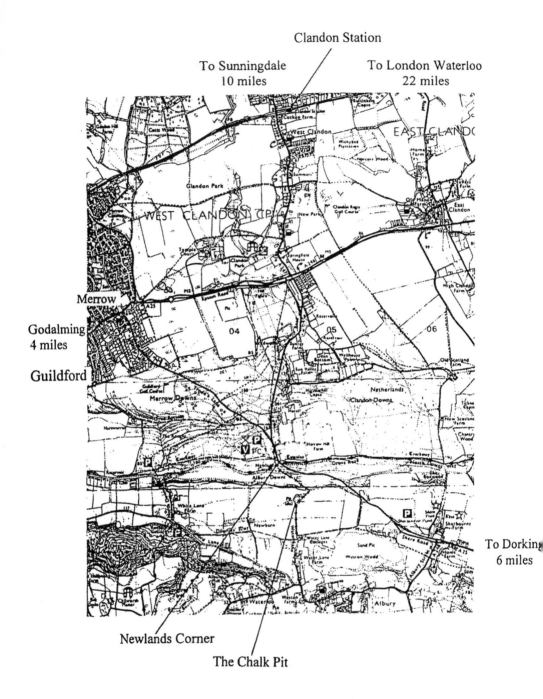

Clandon Station

To Sunningdale
10 miles

To London Waterloo
22 miles

Merrow

Godalming
4 miles

Guildford

To Dorking
6 miles

Newlands Corner

The Chalk Pit

7 Map of Newlands Corner. *After Ordnance Survey*

8 Weekend volunteers engaged in the search. *Photo: Surrey Constabulary*

9 Dragging a river. *Photo: Surrey Constabulary*

10 Surrey Constabulary dog team in search of Agatha. *Photo: Surrey Constabulary*

11 Police officers at the Silent Pool. *Photo*: Daily News, *courtesy Robert Bartlett*

12 Superintendent Charles Goddard. *Photo:*
Wokingham Times

MRS. CHRISTIE DISGUISED.

13 How Agatha may have disguised herself after her disappearance. *Photo*: Daily News, *courtesy Robert Bartlett*

14 A 'Dennis' motor car used by Surrey Constabulary in their reconstruction of the scene of the disappearance. *Photo: Stan Newman*

HURCULACES
ASK FOR
No. 40 for 4d. (per pair)
LUCKY FOR BOOTS
Ask your boot dealer or draper for Hurculaces "No. 40" for Boots and Shoes.

Daily Express

LONDON, MONDAY, DECEMBER 13, 1926.

WEEK-END VOLUNTEERS IN THE HUNT FOR MRS. CHRISTIE.

DOGS JOIN IN THE HUNT.—A Great Dane, and (right) a team of bloodhounds at work at Newlands Corner yesterday, near the spot where Mrs. Christie's motor-car was found.

MRS. AGATHA CHRISTIE, the missing novelist, and (right) a view at Newlands Corner yesterday, thronged with members of the public, who went there to help in the search.

SEARCHERS, who responded to the police appeal for help, setting out yesterday. (Right) Colonel Christie.

WOMEN HELPERS.—A pause for a cigarette. (Right) a woman searcher helped by her dog.

15 *Daily Express:* The Hunt for Agatha.

		Up.													Week Days.															
Miles			mrn	mrn		mrn	mrn		mrn	mrn	mrn	mrn	mrn	mrn	mrn	mrn		mrn	mrn	mrn	mrn	mrn	mrn	mrn	mrn		mrn	mrn	mrn	mrn
	Guildford .....dep.		..	..		..	5 42		..	..	6 28		6 45	..	..	..	7 10	..	7 27	..	7 45	..	..	8 1	..		..	..	8 29
1¼	London Road, Guildford		..	..		..	5 45		..	6 31		6 48	..	..	..	7 13	..	7 30	..	7 48	..	..	8 4	..		..	..	8 32
4¼	Clandon J.		..	..		..	5 51		..	6 37		6 54	..	..	..	7 19	..	7 36	..	7 54	..	..	8 10	..		..	..	8 38
7½	Horsley H.		..	..		..	5 56		..	6 42		6 59	..	..	..	7 24	..	7 41	..	7 59	..	..	8 15	..		..	..	8 43
8¾	Effingham Junction		5 19	..		..	5 59	6 23	6 39	6 48		7 5	7 13	..	7 30	37 7	47	..	8 5	..	8 9	..	..	8 21	..	8 40		8 49
11	Cobham G		..	..		..	6 27		6 52		7 9	..	..	..	7 34	..	7 51	..	8 9	..	..	8 25	..		..	..	8 53
13	Oxshott, for Fairmile		..	..		..	6 30		6 56		7 13	..	..	..	7 38	..	7 55	..	8 13	..	..	8 29	..		..	..	8 57
14¾	Claygate, for Claremont		..	..		..	6 34		7 0		7 17	..	..	..	7 42	..	7 59	..	8 17	..	..	8 33	..		..	..	9 1
—	Mls Hampton Court..dep.		..	5 24		5 50	6 4			7 4		..	..	..	..	..	8 4	..	..	..	..	..		..	..	..
	1 Thames Ditton		..	5 27		5 53	6 7			7 7		..	..	..	..	..	8 7	..	..	..	..	..		..	..	..
18	Surbiton 194.		..	5 31		5 57	6 11	6 40	..	7 6	7 11	7 23	..	..	7 48	..	8 5	8 11	8 23	..	..	8 39	..		..	..	9 7
20¼	Malden, for Coombe		4 25	5 35		6 1	6 15		..	7 15	7 27	..	..	7 53	..	8 9	9 15	..	..	8 43	..		..	8 43
—	Bookham		5 22			..	6 2			6 42		..	..	7 16	..	7 42	..	..	..	8 12	..	..		..	..	8 43
—	Dorking North ..dep.		..			..	6 19		6 59		7 19	..	..	..	..	..	7 57	..	..	8 17	..		..
	Boxhill & Burford B. C		..			..	6 21		7 1		7 21	..	..	..	..	..	7 59	..	..	8 19	..		..
—	Leatherhead 218, 274.		5 25			6 6	6F26	6 46	..	7 6	7 20	7F26	7 46	..	..	..	8 4	8 16	..	6F24	8 47
	Ashtead		5 30			6 10	6 30	6 50	..	7 10		7 30	7 50	..	8 8	8 20	..	8 28	8 51
	Epsom		5 34			6 14	6 34	6 54	..	7 14		7 34	7 54	..	8 14	8 24	..	8 34	8 56
	Ewell West B.		5 37			6 17	6 37	6 57	..	7 17		7 37	7 57	..	8 17	8 27	..	8 37	8 59
	Worcester Park		5 42			6 22	6 42	7 2		7 22		7 42	8 2	..	8 22	8 22	..	8 42	9 6
	Motspur Park		5 44			6 24	6 44	7 4		7 24		7 44	8 4	..	8 24	..	8 44	9 6
21	Raynes Park 198		4 34	5 28	5 48	5 58	6 46	18	6 28	6 48	7 8	7 18	7 28	7 48	8 8	8 18	8 28	8 48	9 10
22½	Wimbledon 207		4 38	5 41	5 51	6 1	6 7	21	6 31	6 48	6 51	7 11	7 14	7 21	7 32	7 31	7 51	8 11	8 14	8 21	8 31	8 31	8 39	8 48	8 51	9 13
24¾	Earlsfield, fr Summerstown		4 43	5 45	5 55	6 5	6 25	35	6 55	7 15	..	7 25		7 35	7 55	8 15	8 25	8 35	8 55	9 17
26	Clapham Junction A		4 48	5 48	5 58	6 8	6 28	38	6 58	7 18	7 18	7 28		7 38	7 58	8 18	8 28	8 38	8 59	9 20
28¼	Vauxhall		4 54	5 53	6 3	6 13	6 33	43	7 3	7 19	7 23	7 23	7 43	..	3	8 3	8 23	8 43	..	9 49	9 25
30	London (Waterloo)....arr.		5 0	5 57	6 7	6 17	6 37	47	6 59	7 7	7 29	7 27	7 25	7 37	7 44	7 47	..	8	7 8	9 8	27 8	25 8	37 8	44 8	47 8	54	..	9 19	8 9	29 9 27

☞ For Notes, see page 193 ; for Continuation of Trains, see pages 192 and 193.

16 Southern Railway Timetable: Clandon to London Waterloo. *Photo: National Railway Museum*

ROYAL BATHS

HARROGATE
IT'S QUICKER BY RAIL

17 *Photo: National Railway Museum*

18 *Photo: National Railway Museum*

18 *Photo: National Railway Museum*

19 *Photo: National Railway Museum*

SUMMARY TABLES
THESE TABLES SHOW THE TRAIN SERVICES BY ALL ROUTES
In some cases alternative higher fares are in operation by routes other than the shortest

LONDON TABLES

LONDON (King's Cross) and BEN RHYDDING, ILKLEY, HARROGATE and RIPON.

		WEEKDAYS *(inc. Saturdays)*		SUNDAYS	
		H .DR|HR J	BC DR|R CG	HR DR FR L H P D	HR. L	H D
			SO	SX SX SO SX		
		a.m. a.m. a.m. a.m. a.m. a.m. p.m p.m	p.m p.m p.m p.m p.m p.m p.m	noon p.m.	p.m.
LONDON (King's Cross)	dep.	4 45 7 15 7 15 10 10 11 20 11 30 1 30 1 40	4 C5 30 5 45 1045 1045 1045 10 45	12 0 10 45	10 45
Ben Rhydding	arr.	10 12 — 12E36 3H36 — 5H15 —	3 52 — 11A47 527 52 —	a.m.	7 52
Ilkley	"	10 15 — 12E59 3N41 — 6H18 —	9 55 — 11A49 557 55	p.m. 7 55	7 55
Harrogate	"	10 44 1K40 1243 2E43 3 3 5 47	5 10 — 8 51 10 9 10E20 4 386 223 5 6 15	5 15 4 38	6 22 8 15
Ripon	"	12 5 1N50 2 39 4 43 3 25	7 11	9 13 — 11A27 5 30 55.5 56 7N54	5 43 5 3	6 55 8 40

		WEEKDAYS		SUNDAYS	
		HR H DR EG ME EFR DR	BC HR. J DR D H SO	HR Y NR	H HS
		a.m. a.m. a.m. a.m. a.m. p.m.	p.m. p.m. p.m. p.m. p.m. p.m. p.m.	a.m. a.m.	a.m. p.m.
Ripon	dep.	— 7 20 7 54 9 0 10 0 1144 124 5	12 58 1 50 2 52 — 7A11 9 20 9 20	— 8 36	9 52 1 15
Harrogate	"	6 30 7 55 8 33 9 35 11 15 1230 12746	1 52 2 45 45 5 8 8 5 3 44 10 35	6 32	10 15 1 45
Ilkley	"	6 14 — 8R12 — 1037 —	2 22 4H 0 — 7 57 —		
Ben Rhydding	"	6 17 — 8H16 . 1040 —	2 25 4H 3 — 8 0 —		
LONDON (King's Cross)	arr.	11 35 1 5 1 35 1 55 3 20 5 10 6 15	4 45 7 22 9 25 10 5 3 35 3 35 3 55	3 45, 5 15	5 55 3 35

A Wednesdays and Saturdays only.
B Pullman Cars only between King's Cross. Harrogate and Ripon. Supplementary charges are made by this train. See page 539.
C Via Church Fenton.
D Via York.
E Via Leeds (Central).
F Through train or carriages between King's Cross and Harrogate.
G Restaurant Car between King's Cross and Harrogate.
H Via Holbeck.
J Restaurant Car between London and Leeds. Through carriages between London and Harrogate.

K On Saturdays arrives Harrogate 12.46 p.m.
L Via Leeds Central and New Stations.
M Pullman Cars only between Harrogate and King's Cross (via Leeds (Central)). Supplementary charges are made by this train (see page 539).
N Via Thirsk and York. P Via York and Leeds (New)
R Restaurant Car.
SO Saturdays only. SX Saturdays excepted.
T On Saturdays leaves Harrogate 1.6 p.m.
Z On Saturdays arrives Harrogate 12.58 p.m. via Leeds (Central). Y Commences 8th May, 1927.

20 LNER Railway Timetable, London King's Cross to Harrogate. *Photo: National Railway Museum*

21 Agatha leaving the Harrogate Hydropathic Hotel on 15 December 1926. *Photo:* Daily Mail

22 'Fuguer' Albert Dadas, sketched by his physician Phillipe Tissié.

THE
MYSTERIOUS AFFAIR
AT STYLES

By AGATHA CHRISTIE

Agatha Christie

A MARY WESTMACOTT NOVEL

UNFINISHED PORTRAIT

25 Superintendent Kenward wearing his King's Police Medal for Gallantry. *Photo: Robert Bartlett*

She would wake up in the night and wander about the house looking for something. One night she knew what it was. She was looking for her mother ... She must find her mother. She dressed and put on a coat and hat. She took her mother's photograph. She would go to the police station and ask them to trace her mother. Her mother had disappeared, but the police would find her ... and once she had found her mother everything would be all right.

She walked for a long time—it was raining and wet ... She couldn't remember what she was walking for. Oh, yes, the police station—where was the police station? Surely in a town, not out in the open country. The police would be kind and helpful. She would give them her mother's name—what was her mother's name? ... Odd, she couldn't remember ... What was her own name? How frightening—she couldn't remember ...[67]

Subconsciously, Agatha had not accepted that her beloved mother Clara, had died.

Dermot's face 'had reminded her of something. Of course! Of the Gun Man! That was the horror of the Gun Man. All the time Dermot had really been the Gun Man ... She felt sick with fear ... She must get home ... she must hide ... The Gun Man was looking for her ... Dermot was stalking her down.

Agatha now associated Archie with the nightmarish character who had terrorised her as a child.

When Celia did finally return home it was 2 o'clock in the morning, and Miss Hood, Judy's governess, was there to comfort her. 'Miss Hood was wonderfully kind and reassuring.' And then reality dawned upon her. 'How stupid, I couldn't have found my mother. I remember—*she's dead* ...'[68]

Miss Hood arranged for the doctor to see Celia and was told by him that his patient was 'in a very grave condition.'[69] Dermot returned, saying 'that he ought to stick to her [Celia] and Judy', and 'that he'd try for three months. He wouldn't even see Marjorie. He said he was sorry'.[70] However, this attempt at reconciliation was a failure. Dermot 'disappeared again—the stranger was here in Dermot's place. He looked at her with hard, hostile eyes ...'.[71]

Archie was now a stranger, and hostile towards Agatha.

She was the Obstacle ... If she were dead ... He wished her dead ... He must wish her dead; otherwise she wouldn't be so afraid.[72]

A rhetorical argument by Agatha, who had convinced herself that Archie wished her dead.

Celia looked in at the nursery door. Judy was sleeping soundly. Celia shut the door noiselessly and came down to the hall and went to the front door. Aubrey [the dog] hurried out of the drawing-room. 'Hallo,' said Aubrey: 'A walk? At this time of night? Well, I don't mind if I do ...'. But his mistress thought otherwise. She took Aubrey's face between her hands and kissed him on the nose. 'Stay at home. Good dog. Can't come with missus.' Can't come with missus—no, indeed! No one must come where missus was going ... She knew now that she couldn't bear any more ... She'd got to escape ...[73]

Agatha's life had become unbearable, and she felt she had to get away from it all. She was presumably in this frame of mind when she decided to 'disappear'.

Miss Hood had gone to London to see her sister come home from abroad. Dermot had seized the opportunity to 'have things out'. He admitted at once he'd been seeing Marjorie. He'd promised—but he hadn't been able to keep the promise.

This implies that, early on the morning of Friday 3 December 1926, Carlo presumably having already departed for London, matters between Agatha and Archie had come to a head (as Jared Cade suggested).

She had said when he had explained that he was going away but would come back two days later: 'You won't find me here.' By the flicker in his eyelids she had felt sure he knew what she meant ...[74]

The inference is that, prior to Agatha's disappearance, Archie had announced that he would be spending the weekend away from home—i.e. with Nancy Neele, whereupon Agatha threatened to leave home.

[Dermot] wouldn't accept facts as they were—he wanted things to be as he would like them to be. But death *was* a solution ...[75]

It wasn't as though he'd feel himself to blame for it [i.e. her suicide]. He would soon persuade himself that Celia had been in a bad way ever since the death of her mother. Dermot was so clever at persuading himself ...[76]

She no longer thought of Judy—she had got past that ... Nothing mattered to her now but her own agony and her longing for escape ...

Finally, Celia climbed up on a parapet above a river and jumped.[77]

The inference is that Agatha was so depressed that her only thought was to do away with herself, which, by her own account, she attempted to achieve by driving her car over the edge of a chalk pit.

Having failed in her attempt and been rescued from the river, Celia had no further thoughts of suicide, but she felt ashamed about having abandoned Judy.[78]

Shame was undoubtedly what Agatha, as the mother of Rosalind, would have felt after her own flight from home.

Finally, when Dermot wrote to Celia enclosing the necessary evidence to enable the divorce to take place, which in those days meant evidence of adultery, Celia obliged by divorcing him.[79] And within a few days of the decree being made absolute, he married Marjorie Connell.[80]

On 29 October 1928, Agatha's divorce from Archie was finalised. That December, Archie married Nancy Neele.

In conclusion, Larraby, having come to the rescue of Celia, declared that:

The danger was over. It was as though the burden had been taken from her shoulders and laid on mine. She was safe ...[81]

It is my fixed belief that Celia went back into the world to begin a new life ... She went back at thirty-nine—to grow up ... And she left her story and her fear—with me ...[82]

* * *

In *Unfinished Portrait*, it is clear that Agatha had herself in mind when she invented the character 'Celia'. Both Celia and Agatha's fathers died before they (the girls) reached their teenage years. Like

Agatha, Celia found her mother Miriam to be a great comfort to her. Dermot, like Archie, liked to 'get his own way'. And just as Celia confessed to being afraid of Dermot, so Agatha's letter to Superintendent Kenward implied that she feared that Archie might murder her. Dermot disliked the physical side of their relationship and, in Celia's eyes, failed to give her emotional support, unlike her mother Miriam, who gave her love and made her feel 'adequate'. When Miriam died, Celia felt totally alone and in a panic. The husbands of both Celia and Agatha were unfaithful, and demanded that their wives consent to a divorce.

Moreover, the strain of the situation led to a deterioration in Celia's health, and all the more so when Dermot came to personify the nightmare of Agatha's childhood dreams—the Gun Man. Having convinced herself that Dermot wished her dead, Celia, like Agatha, decided to 'run away' from the 'empty' house. Celia attempted suicide, and Agatha implied that so too did she—and both survived. Whereupon Celia felt ashamed at having abandoned her daughter Judy, in the same way as Agatha, without doubt, felt a similar shame at having abandoned Rosalind.

Given that, in *Unfinished Portrait*, the life of Celia mirrors that of Agatha in very many ways, it is difficult to conceive of any reason why Agatha should have based half the book on her lifetime's experiences and invented the other half, so full as it was of pain and pathos. Instead, the obvious conclusion is that she took the opportunity, writing under the pseudonym Mary Westmacott, to describe precisely what the problems were in her marriage and what drove her ultimately to despair, which culminated in the suicide attempt at Newlands Corner. Agatha's second husband, Max Mallowan, appeared to share this view when he said of *Unfinished Portrait* that, 'In Celia we have more nearly than anywhere else a portrait of Agatha.'[83]

For Agatha, the writing of the novel was a catharsis, whereby she forced herself to confront her past in its entirety, no matter how painful the process may have been for her, in the hope that, having done so, she could put it behind her.

Was Agatha's portrayal of Archie, both in her autobiography and obliquely in *Unfinished Portrait*, in which he appeared as 'Dermot', a fair one? Those who are in love and who find their plans frustrated may resort to desperate measures, but it is difficult to think of Archie as a potential wife murderer.

Whatever the truth of the matter, what can be said for certain is that, on the night of her disappearance, Agatha appeared to have convinced herself: a) that her life had become unbearable; b) that Archie wished her dead; c) that she must escape from the position in which she found herself. However, in *Unfinished Portrait*, Celia was so depressed as to feel that the only remaining option was for her to take her own life, which she attempted to do. But is Agatha to be believed, when she proclaimed her 'intention of doing something desperate', stated how, 'That night I felt terribly miserable. I felt that I could go on no longer,' and announced that she had bruised her head and chest in the car crash? Or had she deliberately left her car perched on the cliff top above the chalk pit in order to give the *impression* that she, like Celia, had attempted suicide, when in fact, she had not?

Agatha stated that the only person who guessed that *Unfinished Portrait* was written, not by 'Mary Westmacott' but by herself, was Nan Kon[84] (a fact which was not generally known until 1949 when it was revealed by the *Sunday Times*). This was apart from Max Mallowan, of course, as indicated above. Does it therefore follow that Max was aware that, almost four years prior to their wedding, Agatha had made a suicide attempt? The answer must, almost certainly, be yes.

CHAPTER 15

Agatha's Real Life Saviour

In *Unfinished Portrait*, Celia met Larraby, her 'saviour', who took away her burden for her. The question now arises, did Agatha herself have a similar experience, following her divorce from Archie, whereby a real-life 'saviour' came to *her* rescue?

In her autobiography Agatha described how, whilst on holiday on the island of Las Palmas, where she had stayed with Rosalind and Carlo in January/February 1927,[1] she met a Dr Lucas and his sister Mrs Meek.[2] Further details of Dr Lucas, the proverbial 'knight in shining armour' who rescued Agatha, the 'damsel in distress', are to be found in *The Medical Directory* for the year 1927.[3] His first name was Geoffrey, his address: Cook's Hill, Mundesley, Norfolk, and his telephone number: 'Mundesley 4'. Having studied at Cambridge, Durham, and St George's Hospital, London, and having worked at the Nordrach Sanatorium, Banchory near Aberdeen, Scotland, he was currently Resident Physician at the Mundesley Sanatorium. (This was without doubt the 'sanatorium on the east coast' to which Agatha referred in her autobiography; Mundesley being situated on the coast of Norfolk, about 18 miles from its county town of Norwich.)

From Agatha's account, Dr Lucas was a man of great kindness and humanity. He was also a distinguished physician—being a Fellow of the Royal Society of Medicine—whose published papers included *Climate of Deeside*;[4] *Treatment of Dry Pleurisy by Temporary Partial Artificial Pneumothorax*; and *Treatment of Pulmonary Tuberculosis by Nitrogen Compression*.[5]

Dr Lucas, whom Agatha referred to as 'Father', was 'by nature a born healer', who became a friend and comfort to her.[6] Could it be that it was Dr Lucas who Agatha had in mind when she created the portrait painter 'Larraby'? And was Dr Lucas himself something of an amateur painter? Who knows?

CHAPTER 16

Jared Cade and the Testimony of the Gardners

In *Agatha Christie and the Eleven Missing Days*, published in 1998, Jared Cade, the author, revealed some startling information in respect of Agatha's disappearance.

> Nan Watts was Madge's sister-in-law and life-long friend, and Nan's daughter and son-in-law, Judith and Graham Gardner, have confirmed the truth about the disappearance and other hitherto undisclosed details of Agatha's personal life.[1]

In fact, Judith, born in December 1916, was Nan's daughter by her first husband Hugo Pollock, whom she had married in 1912. Judith was only 10 years old at the time of Agatha's disappearance.[2] This marriage ended in divorce, and in 1926 Nan married George Kon, a distinguished professor of chemistry. Continued Cade:

> When the Gardners met me in 1997 they decided it was time for the truth to be told, especially as Judith's mother, Nan, had been directly involved.[3] Judith and Graham knew Agatha intimately, and their knowledge of her together [i.e. jointly] spans over eighty-five years.[4]

And now came the punch line. It was Nan Kon who had helped Agatha 'to orchestrate the disappearance'.[5] Furthermore, according to Cade, Graham Gardner asked Nan directly, 'if she had helped Agatha disappear', whereupon Nan:

> admitted her involvement in the affair and added with admirable aplomb, 'What does it matter after all this time?'[6]

This statement by Nan was made some time after Agatha's second marriage, on 11 September 1930, to Max Mallowan.

When Cade met with and interviewed the Gardners in 1997, this was more than seven decades after Agatha's disappearance in 1926, and almost four decades after Nan's death (in 1959) at the age of 71 (when Judith was aged 43). Judith was now aged 81 and Graham 83. What credence, if any, may therefore be placed on the above evidence provided by the Gardners and narrated by Cade?

In *Agatha Christie and the Eleven Missing Days*, Cade, again presumably drawing on what the Gardners had told him, stated that:

On the morning of her disappearance [Friday 3 December] the couple had their worst row ever. During the row Archie made it clear that he had no intention of accompanying Agatha to Beverley in Yorkshire for the weekend, as she hoped he would. He then told her he could not stand the charade of their attempted reconciliation any longer. Deeply shaken, she accused him of seeing Nancy behind her back. He admitted that he had made plans to spend the weekend with his mistress and that he had decided, once and for all, to marry her. Their argument ended with Archie storming off to work.[7]

In the light of what is known about the fraught and precarious state of Agatha's marriage, this account is entirely credible, and if true, then surely this row was the final straw which convinced Agatha that she must leave home.

According to Cade, on the evening of Tuesday 14 December, when Archie and Agatha were dining together at The Harrogate Hydro, having been reunited with one another, they were joined by a Mr Alexander Pettleson, who reported on the couple's conversation as follows:

After their row on the morning of the disappearance she [Agatha] had driven up to London to confide her problems to the one person whom she knew would understand[8] [i.e. Nan Kon]. Nan had moved to 78 Chelsea Park Gardens, and Agatha had been in a dreadful state when she had arrived there on Friday morning.[9]

Did Agatha pay a visit to Nan Kon on that Friday morning, as Cade suggested? By his own admission, Archie left home that morning at 9.15 a.m. Assuming that Agatha had set off by car for London at about the same time, and had returned to Styles in time for lunch (as stated by both Archie and Gwen Robyns)—i.e. say, by 1 p.m., or 2 p.m. at the latest, bearing in mind that in the afternoon, she visited her mother-in-law Mrs Helmsley in Dorking,[10] then this means that she would have been absent from home for a maximum of five to six hours. The distance from Sunningdale to Chelsea (where Nan lived) is 22 miles, and the two districts were linked by 'Class 1' designated roads (i.e. main roads leading from one major centre of population to another; later known as 'A' roads). So a journey of 44 miles at an average speed of 15 mph would have taken about three hours, and at an average speed of 10 mph, about four hours. Time wise, it would therefore have been feasible for Agatha to have met with Nan that morning, when the two ladies would have had two or three hours of time to spend together (or more time, if Agatha had set off even earlier that morning). As for Rosalind, did she accompany Agatha, or was she left behind with no Carlo and only the remaining household staff to look after her?

Agatha had previously told Archie, continued Cade:

that she had confided to Nan that she was thinking of doing something desperate if he went ahead with his plans to leave her for Nancy.

This is in accordance with Agatha's statement to the *Daily Mail*, that when she left home that Friday night, it was 'with the intention of doing something desperate'.[11]

Agatha revealed that she had spoken to Nan of abandoning her car at Newlands Corner because it was only a few miles from Hurstmore Cottage, and she wanted the car's discovery to disrupt his [Archie's] weekend with Nancy and lead to three or four days of very unpleasant questioning by the police, who she hoped would suspect him of murdering her.[12]

If Agatha's motive *was* to embarrass Archie and make him a murder suspect, then she certainly achieved her aim. Meanwhile, according to Cade, Sam James, the host, declared that 'the party' which had assembled at Hurstmore Cottage, Godalming, 'consisted of my wife [Madge], a Miss Neele, the Colonel [Archie] and myself'.[13] This account tallies with a statement made by Gwen Robyns.

How close a relationship did Agatha have with Nan Kon, who was almost two years her senior and whom she had known since childhood? Very close, according to Agatha. There was, practically, no one else but Nan with whom she could reminisce about Abney Hall, the Watts' home in Cheshire, and Ashfield, Agatha's own family home; of their pet dogs; the 'pranks' that they got up to; the young men who courted them, and the plays which they 'got up and acted in'.[14] Given these circumstances, it would therefore have been only natural for Agatha to have confided in her sister-in-law. However, said Agatha, after Nan's marriage in 1912 to the wealthy Hugo Pollock,[15] and Nan's move to London:

> I felt rather diffident about approaching her. This sounds silly, and indeed it *was* silly, but one cannot pretend that differences in income do not separate people.[16]

Agatha did, however, refer to a weekend when Nan and her second husband, George Kon, came to stay at Sunningdale when 'George and Archie played golf together'.[17] Continued Cade, it was therefore:

> agreed that if Agatha went ahead with her scheme she could spend the night [of Friday 3 December] with her [Nan], since her second husband George Kon was away. The two women had decided that Agatha [after her disappearance] should claim to be suffering from amnesia when she was found, because it would later release her from awkward explanations.[18]

When Agatha revealed this to Archie, allegedly when they were having dinner together at The Hydro on the evening of Tuesday 14 December, he:

> was staggered, because Nan had given everyone to understand she was as upset over Agatha's inexplicable absence as the rest of her family.[19]

Said Cade, shortly after 9.45 p.m. on the night of Friday 3 December, Agatha had:

> driven directly to Newlands Corner, where she had let the car roll off the plateau with the handbrake off and the gears in neutral. She had intentionally left the headlights on to draw attention to the car, and her fur coat, an attaché case of clothes and her driver's licence had been left inside so that it would look as if something untoward had happened.[20]

This reference to the gears and handbrake is in accordance with Frederick Dore's statement, as reported by *The Times*, that when the car was discovered, its 'brakes were off and it was in neutral'.[21] However, Cade's assertion that 'the main reason she left her fur coat on the back seat of her car is because it would have been too hot for walking in', simply does not make sense, given that it was the depth of winter and the ambient temperature was barely above freezing.[22]

Cade then suggests that Agatha walked to West Clandon [i.e. Clandon] Station and caught the 10.52 p.m. train to London.[23]

> When Agatha had arrived at 78 Chelsea Park Gardens later than night, Nan had been half expecting her and had not been at all surprised to learn that Archie had gone ahead with his plans to spend the weekend with Nancy.[24]

This theory of Cade's, however, does not tally either with Agatha's own account, or with those of Edward McAlister and Frederick Dore, and it must therefore be discounted.

Again, as already mentioned, Agatha's estimated time of arrival at Waterloo Station was some time between 8.25 a.m. and 9.01 a.m. She would therefore have had at least four hours to make her way from there to King's Cross, a distance of two miles, (presumably by taxicab), there to catch the 1.40 p.m. train to Harrogate. This would have allowed sufficient time for her to have met with Nan Kon, as Cade alleged.

> On Saturday morning, before Agatha left London, the two women had visited the Army and Navy Department Store in Victoria.

Laura Thompson also mentioned that Agatha took a taxi from Waterloo Station to the Army and Navy Stores, but neither she nor Janet Morgan (both of whom had access to the Christie archive) made any mention of a meeting with Nan Kon, or of Agatha having stayed overnight with Nan.[25]

At the Army and Navy Stores, continued Cade:

> Nan gave Agatha money to acquire some items of clothing and other articles and a small case to take to Harrogate with her, since the clothes she had packed in her attaché case the previous night had been left behind in her abandoned car. They had rung two or three of the best-known hotels in Harrogate to see which had vacancies and after discovering none were full owing to the [pre-] Christmas lull, had decided that Agatha should just turn up at the Harrogate Hydro since this would later support her claim of having lost her memory.[26]
>
> After they had lunch together, Nan had given Agatha some more money, then Agatha had caught the 1.40 p.m. train from King's Cross, which arrived in Harrogate at 6.40 p.m. [According to the railway timetable, this train, as already mentioned, was scheduled to arrive at Harrogate, not at 6.40 p.m., but half-an-hour earlier, at 6.10 p.m..]

Finally:

> she had taken a taxi from Harrogate Station and, a little before seven o'clock, had booked into Room 105 of the Harrogate Hydro as Mrs Teresa Neele of Cape Town, South Africa.[27]

Other assertions made by Cade

Although the Harrogate police contacted Superintendent Kenward on Monday 13 December about this possible sighting of Agatha, said Cade, 'he, not believing in the substance of their claims, failed to pass on the information to the Berkshire police or to the household at Styles', until he was again contacted by the West Riding [of Yorkshire] police on the morning of Tuesday 14 December. And it was only then, 'around midday' that Kenward telephoned Styles.[28]

But Gwen Robyns stated that:

It was just after 9 a.m. on Tuesday December 14, that Deputy Chief Constable Kenward tried to telephone Colonel Christie at his home Styles, and was told that the Colonel had just left for his office in London.[29]

Cade states that Agatha, in her novel *Unfinished Portrait*, 'avoids examining the reasons behind the breakdown of the marriage …'[30] In fact, as has been amply demonstrated, Agatha, vicariously through the characters in her novel, provides *a wealth of clues* as to what these reasons might have been.

CHAPTER 17

Unanswered Questions

What was in Agatha's mind when she departed from Styles?

Agatha, by her own admission to the *Daily Mail:*

> left home that night [Friday 3 December] in a state of high nervous strain with the intention of doing something desperate. I just wanted my life to end. That night I felt terribly miserable. I felt that I could go on no longer.[1]

Why did she choose to leave home at 10 p.m.?

This was presumably for Rosalind's sake, in order to minimize the time between her [Agatha's] departure and the return of Carlo; though the remaining household staff could doubtless have coped in an emergency.

Was her departure pre-planned?

The fact that Carlo had been given the day off suggests that Agatha's departure from Styles was pre-planned, for, had her secretary been present at the time, she would undoubtedly have remonstrated with her and tried to dissuade her from driving off into the night. Also, Carlo would have insisted on knowing where Agatha intended to go, and what she intended to do; facts which Agatha was anxious to keep secret from her secretary, as the letter that she left for Carlo indicated.

The contents of Agatha's car

Janet Morgan pointed out how odd it was that someone who intended to kill themselves should have taken the trouble to 'pack a nightgown,'[2] as well as, it might also be said, several items of clothing, and spare pairs of shoes? But this ignores the fact that when Agatha set out, it was probably her original intention to go to Yorkshire.

Did Agatha meet with Archie that Friday night, after departing from Styles?

If so, then the Newlands Corner Hotel would have been the ideal place for a rendezvous, and, in particular, the hotel's comfortable lounge or elegant library. However, if Agatha is to be believed, when she stated that she drove to London and Maidenhead before returning to Sunningdale and motoring on to Newlands Corner, then this would have added an extra 24 miles—or one and a half to two and a half hours to her journey—excluding the time spent with Archie. This diversion, as will be seen, was therefore hardly possible within the known time frame.

Gwen Robyns quotes a statement Sam James of Hurstmore Cottage made to the *Daily Mail*, *which corroborates this view.*

> Suggestions have been made that Colonel Christie was called up by his wife while he was here [i.e. on the night of Friday 3 December], or that he went out and met his wife, or that she came here to meet him. Nothing of the kind happened.[3]

Therefore, any possibility that Agatha met with Archie that Friday night can almost certainly be discounted.

What really happened on that Friday/Saturday night?

Cade's theory that Agatha had spent the night of 3–4 December with Nan Kon (which was presumably based on what he had been told by Judith and Graham Gardner) contradicts Agatha's own account, in which she stated that she drove around in her car for most of that time. It also flies in the face of the statement made by Superintendent Kenward to A. L. Dixon of the Home Office, that he had personally 'interviewed a man named McAlister who stated that at 6.20 a.m.' on the morning of Saturday 4 December, 'he had helped a lady, whose description was identical with that of Mrs Christie, to start the engine of the car found'.[4] These last three words, 'the car found', are highly significant, in that they confirm that Kenward had no doubt whatsoever in his mind that the car which McAlister had described was the one which was later found abandoned—i.e. Agatha's grey, four-seater Morris Cowley, and that the lady in distress was Agatha herself. Furthermore, McAlister had nothing to gain by inventing such a story, except perhaps a little local glory, and a great deal to lose—the penalties for giving false evidence to the police being very severe in those days.

Assuming, for a moment, that Agatha did drive directly to Nan's and spent the night there; then drove to Newlands Corner early the following morning. This would have entailed a journey of about 70 miles in total. If so, given an average speed of 15 mph, it would have taken her about four and a half hours, leaving less than four hours for sleep and socialising. The proposition is, therefore, highly unlikely.

Or, having arrived at Nan's home, did Agatha hand her car over to an accomplice, who drove it to Newlands Corner and abandoned it there? If so, bearing in mind that Edward McAlister described encountering a lady, at 6.20 a.m. that Saturday morning, 'whose description was identical with that of Mrs Christie',[5] then this accomplice must have been disguised to look exactly like Agatha! But neither Janet Morgan nor Laura Thompson made any mention of Agatha having met with Nan on that Saturday morning, despite having been granted full access to Agatha's correspondence, which implies that they discovered no evidence to this effect.

Therefore, Agatha's own explanation of her movements during the night of 3–4 December is the most persuasive—i.e., that she drove to London, then Maidenhead, then Sunningdale, and finally

Newlands Corner. The question is, was it possible for her to have made this journey, in the time available?

The length of the journey, described as above by Agatha and undertaken on the night of 3–4 December, was as follows. Sunningdale to Euston Station, 24 miles; Euston Station to Maidenhead, 26 miles; Maidenhead to London, 26 miles; London to Sunningdale, 20 miles; Sunningdale to Newlands Corner, 12 miles. During the course of the night the Morris Cowley, therefore, would have covered a distance of about 110 miles. Furthermore, almost the entire journey could have been accomplished using none other than 'Class 1' designated roads.

The question is, was it possible for Agatha to have completed such a journey between the time she left home at 10 p.m. on the Friday evening, and 6.20 a.m. the following morning, when she was seen in the vicinity of Newlands Corner by Edward McAlister—i.e. a period of just under eight and a half hours?

A contemporary motoring guide stated as follows:

> It has been said that in these days it is safer to drive a car after dark than in the daytime, providing the weather is fine and the roads are dry, because of the greatly reduced number of vehicles using the roads, for one thing, and also because, at cross roads and corners, the presence of approaching vehicles is better indicated by their headlamps at night than by the sound of their horns in daytime.

Records reveal that when Agatha set off that night, the weather was mainly clear, with some mist and dew, and a light, north-westerly wind blowing across southern England. However, as the night wore on, the sky clouded over and there was a ground frost. The minimum temperature was one degree centigrade, but the strength of the wind would have increased the chill factor.[6]

> Special care is, nevertheless, needed when driving at night. On country roads, for instance, the severity of corners is often deceptive; even one's approach to them may not be realized soon enough to enable the car speed to be reduced to a really safe figure, unless one is constantly on the *qui vive*. In town areas, special caution is needed because of the partial dazzle arising from street lamps; the possibility of side turnings being overlooked, and other vehicles issuing from them unexpectedly.[7]
>
> The dazzling effect of oncoming headlights can be very largely avoided by the driver refraining from looking at the approaching lamps. If the dazzling is so severe that not even the nearside edge of the road can be seen, there is nothing to be done but reduce the speed to a mere crawl, or even stop.[8]

It might also be necessary to reduce speed in towns, in order to negotiate tram rails, in which the wheels of a vehicle might become lodged; and in the countryside, livestock such as sheep and cattle might be encountered on the roads.

> For the present… the legal limit of speed remains at 20 mph, except in those places where a lower limit has been set by the local authorities with the consent of the Local Government Board, or the Ministry of Transport. These lower speed limits are usually 10 mph and the area to which they apply is indicated by special signs.
>
> It need hardly be said that the 20 mph limit is far more honoured in the breach than in the observance by every motorist, and although 'traps' are set in various places from time to time, the police are more or

less indulgent, instituting prosecutions, when they consider it advisable to do so, for furious, dangerous, or reckless driving rather than for merely exceeding the speed limit.[9]

Assuming that Agatha was a law-abiding citizen and kept within the speed limits, her average speed for such a journey is estimated to have been in the region of about 15 miles per hour. (The then maximum speed for the 1925–26 Morris Cowley was stated as 50–52 m.p.h. in the sales catalogue; though this may have been a somewhat optimistic figure!)[10]

However, according to Laura Thompson, it was stated in the *Westminster Gazette* that:

Agatha could drive to London in fifty-five minutes: from Sunningdale to the centre is about twenty-five miles.

In other words, she was capable of making the journey, presumably during daylight hours, at an average speed of 27 mph—which was 7 mph in excess of the maximum legal speed limit!

Furthermore, for a car of that engine capacity—i.e. 1548 cc, 'a gallon of petrol should be sufficient for about 35 miles'.[11] However, according to Morris Cowley owner Malcolm McKay, 30 miles per gallon is a more realistic figure, and as the capacity of the petrol tank was five gallons, with an auxiliary two-gallon can attached to the running board behind the spare wheel, there would have been no necessity for Agatha to stop to refuel, provided that she had started with a full tank. In practice, because garages, like shops, were only open during the daytime, there would have been no possibility of refuelling during the night, in any event.

It was, therefore, possible for Agatha to have completed the entire journey of 110 miles comfortably in about eight hours, barring mishaps, and including extra time added on for stops (i.e. at Euston Station and at Maidenhead).

Finally, given the fact that the petrol tanks must have been full or thereabouts, does this indicate that Agatha envisaged embarking on a long journey before she set off? Or was it simply that she was in the habit of keeping the car well topped up with fuel?

Why Newlands Corner?

The possibilities are as follows:

1. Agatha selected Newlands Corner with the deliberate intention of committing suicide by driving her car over the edge of the chalk pit. However, her statement that 'as I passed by Newlands Corner that afternoon I saw a quarry' is difficult to explain, because although the road on which she would have travelled—the A25—passed within about 260 yards of the chalk pit, it would not have been visible to her owing to the convex shape of the hill. This begs the question; had Agatha visited the area on a previous occasion, either at leisure, or in order to reconnoitre the site? In other words, was it already in her mind that the chalk pit at Newlands Corner would be a suitable spot at which to commit suicide?

It seems strange that Agatha should choose to drive her car over the edge of a chalk pit, when there was no certainty that this would have had the desired effect—i.e. her death—and that, instead, she might be left severely injured, and perhaps disabled for the rest of her life. Surely, the taking of poison would have been a far more reliable way of ending her life, and of course since the days when she worked at Torquay Hospital's pharmaceutical dispensary, Agatha had both a fascination for and knowledge of poisons.

2. Having almost completed her long, night-time journey, Agatha decided to pay a visit to Dorking (ten miles further along the A25 from Newlands Corner), in order to make a final appeal for help to her mother-in-law Mrs Helmsley. However, she changed her mind and decided to abort her journey at Newlands Corner? (Had she been *en route* to Godalming to confront Archie, she would have taken the A320 from Woking, and not the A247–A25). But there is no evidence for this hypothesis.

3. Agatha made a calculated decision to abandon her car at Newlands Corner in order to cause maximum embarrassment to Archie–this being only five miles distant from Godalming, where her husband was spending the weekend with his mistress. After all, as Laura Thompson pointed out, 'Why should Agatha have abandoned her car so near to Godalming, if she had not been thinking directly of Archie?'[12] But why, if this was the case, was the vehicle discovered virtually overhanging a quarry? Why had she not simply abandoned it in the lane?

A genuine attempt at suicide?

According to Agatha, she set off from Styles that Friday evening:

> in a state of high nervous strain with the intention of doing something desperate. I drove in my car over the crest of the Downs in the direction of a quarry. The car struck something and I was flung against the steering wheel and injured my chest and head.[13]

These statements could hardly have been more explicit. Yes, this was a genuine attempt at suicide.

The alleged injury to Agatha's head

Agatha stated that the injury to her chest and head were caused by their impact with the steering wheel of the car. But if Agatha's head had struck the steering wheel, then surely bruises would have been visible subsequently, on her face; since, judging by the damage sustained by the car, which was significant, it may be deduced that the force of the impact was fairly substantial. However, of the many people at The Hydro with whom she came in contact, not one makes any mention of this.

However, those who are familiar with road traffic accidents know that, in the days before the invention of seatbelts, the tendency in a head-on collision is for the body of the occupant of the motor vehicle to be propelled upwards and forwards. In other words, Agatha's head would have come into contact with the roof of the car. As for the bruises to her chest, these may have been caused by the steering wheel, as her body fell back down into the seat. It is therefore likely that it was the top of Agatha's head that was bruised, and that the bruise was invisible as it was covered by her hair.

It should also be remembered that Agatha may have closed her eyes, just prior to the impact, and been dazed by it, so that, when she came to, she deduced, mistakenly, that the steering wheel was the principal cause of her injuries.

Impact with the bush

The fact that the car had impacted with the bush may indicate a) that Agatha was a bad driver, b) that she did not notice the bush in the darkness of the night, c) that there was a line of bushes, leaving her with no option but to attempt to plough through them, and on into the chalk pit or: d) that she deliberately left the car in this position, to give the false impression that this was a suicide attempt—which, if this was the case, would provide an opportunity for her beloved Morris Cowley to be recovered at some later date.

A deliberate deception on Agatha's part?

Laura Thompson, however, who was sceptical of Agatha's account, believed that, prior to the car crash, Agatha 'got out of the car' and then 'pushed hard and the car rolled smack into the bush…'.[14] It will also be recalled that according to *The Times*, the car's discoverer, Frederick Dore, stated that 'the position of the car suggested to him that it must have been given a push at the top of the hill and sent down deliberately'.[15] Both these points of view, however, are purely conjectural.

Agatha's subsequent amnesia

For a period of 24 hours following her car crash, Agatha complained of memory loss. If, as seems likely, she was at the wheel of the car when it struck the bushes above the chalk pit at Newlands Corner, then it is possible that she was temporarily concussed, principally due to the impact of her head with the vehicle's roof (concussion **being defined** as 'temporary unconsciousness or confusion … caused by a blow on the head').[16] However, bearing in mind that she left the scene within one and a half hours at most of the car crash (i.e. between 6.20 a.m. when McAlister helped her and 8 a.m. when the vehicle was found abandoned by Dore), then any such concussion must have worn off fairly quickly, as she was sufficiently conscious to make her way to the nearest railway station, and from there to London.

Also, in 'post-concussional disorder', symptoms include impaired concentration and post-traumatic amnesia, whereby, for a period following the head injury, the person is unable to store new information. In addition, for such a diagnosis to be made, three or more of the following disorders must be present for at least three months:

> Becoming fatigued easily; disordered sleep; headache; vertigo or dizziness; irritability or aggression on little or no provocation; anxiety, depression, or affective lability [mood swings]; changes in personality; apathy or lack of spontaneity.[17]

However, her energetic and gregarious behaviour at The Hydro contrasts strongly with the picture of post-concussional disorder painted above. It is therefore unlikely that the head injury sustained by Agatha in the crash was of sufficient severity to have caused the 24-hour period of amnesia of which she complained. Neither can it explain the bizarre behaviour displayed by her at the Harrogate Hydro and thereafter, nor the fact that her amnesia persisted, to a degree, for many years.

CHAPTER 18

The Aftermath of the Car Crash:
The Journey from Newlands Corner to Harrogate

The question arises, how did Agatha manage to accomplish the journey from Newlands Corner to London?

The Aldershot & District Bus Company ran a small fleet of omnibuses between various towns in the vicinity, but it is likely that the service was an infrequent one. On the other hand, Agatha would have been well aware of the location of Clandon railway station, having passed it many times on her way from Sunningdale to Dorking.

Tom Roberts and Jared Cade have suggested, as already mentioned, that she walked from Newlands Corner to the railway station at Clandon—a distance of about two and a quarter miles along the A25 main road, which could easily be covered within the space of an hour. And here, local knowledge would come in useful, for, as Mrs Helmsley said, Agatha 'knew the roads so well and even in the dark she would not lose her way'. Even so, trudging alone across the lonely downland in the darkness of the night must have seemed a daunting prospect. (As already mentioned, twilight that morning did not commence until 7.10 a.m. and sunrise was at 7.48 a.m.)

Agatha was last seen in the vicinity of Newlands Corner at 6.20 a.m. that Saturday morning (by Edward McAlister), and her vehicle was found abandoned at Newlands Corner at 8 a.m. (by Frederick Dore). One may conclude, therefore, that she set off, on foot, at some time between, say, 6.30 a.m. and 7.50 a.m., and arrived at Clandon station at some time between 7.30 a.m. and 8.30 a.m.

En route from Newlands Corner to Clandon station, Agatha would have passed Newlands Corner Hotel, a pumping station, a church with rectory, two public houses, almshouses and several private dwellings. The question is, why did she not stop at any of these locations and ask for help—which she evidently did not? This again indicates, not a woman in severe distress who has just attempted suicide, but instead, a person who is implementing a premeditated plan.

Given the weather conditions, and without the benefit of a coat, she must have been half frozen and suffering from exposure when she arrived at Clandon station, not to say exhausted through lack of sleep. From here, trains were scheduled to depart at 7.36 a.m., 7.54 a.m., and 8.10 a.m.; arriving at London Waterloo at 8.25 a.m., 8.44 a.m., and 9.01 a.m. respectively.[1]

From King's Cross to Harrogate

The *Harrogate Advertiser* reported that Agatha had 'arrived at The Hydro late in the afternoon of Saturday December 4th', but in the same article, declared that she had arrived 'on Saturday night, December 4th'.[2] Jared Cade was, therefore, probably correct in stating that Agatha had caught the

.40 p.m. train from King's Cross, which was scheduled to arrive at Harrogate at 6.10 p.m. (and not, as he stated, at 6.40 p.m.). Add another twenty minutes or so, for the journey from the station to the Hydro, and this gives a time of arrival of about 6.30 p.m.

Why did Agatha select Harrogate as her destination, having cancelled her hotel reservation at Beverley?

According to Janet Morgan, this was because, 'at Waterloo Station she [Agatha] saw a poster advertising the spa at Harrogate'.[3]

The London and North Eastern Railway Company (LNER) produced posters advertising various destinations throughout the country as prospective holiday resorts and, even though Waterloo Station was the terminus for the Southern Railway, it is likely that LNER had a representative at Waterloo, and displayed its posters there.[4]

Two dozen or more such posters were produced by the LNER advertising Harrogate alone, and depicting various aspects of the town. One, for example, bore the caption

Harrogate: Its Quicker by Rail.
Free Guide from Publicity Manager, Royal Baths, Harrogate.
Full information from any LNER office or agency.

Another, and perhaps the most alluring, advertised as follows

THE ROYAL HALL
HARROGATE VIA LNER
Come for Health—Stay for Pleasure
FREE BROCHURE FROM F. J. C. BROOME HARROGATE OR ANY LNER AGENCY

This may, in fact, have been *the very poster which had caught Agatha's eye. (Mr Broome was General Manager of Harrogate's Royal Baths, as will shortly be seen.) Harrogate was, therefore, the ideal place for Agatha to rest, recuperate, and also obtain treatment for her neuritis.*

At The Hydro

What possessed Agatha to adopt the name 'Teresa Neele'? And what possessed her to place an advertisement in *The Times*, inviting friends and relatives of that fictitious lady to contact her? Surely, even if Archie had noticed the advertisement, it was hardly likely that he would have associated 'Teresa Neele, late of South Africa' with his wife Agatha! Or was this intended to be a coded signal to Nan Kon, and perhaps to others who were privy to the fact that she was now operating under the name of 'Neele'? If so, then why not simply telephone Nan, or write a letter? Or was there an altogether different explanation?

CHAPTER 19

Agatha's Fascination with the Themes of 'Infidelity', ' Disappearance', Amnesia, and 'Change of Identity'

As already mentioned, Agatha, prior to her disappearance, had spoken to Archie about the possibility that she might disappear, and it is therefore not surprising that this theme, together with that of memory loss and change of identity, should feature in some of her works of fiction.

The Secret Adversary (1922)

In 1922, four years prior to her disappearance, Agatha's novel *The Secret Adversary*, was published. Jane Finn, who was a passenger on the real-life ocean liner *Lusitania*, suffered a severe shock 'when that ill-fated ship was sunk' by a German submarine on the afternoon of 7 May 1915.[1] She now experienced:

> a complete loss of memory. She did not know her own name, or where she had come from, or where she was. She couldn't even speak her own tongue.

The first thing she did remember was 'landing with the survivors'.[2]

According to criminal lawyer 'Sir James Peel Edgerton', who also featured in the story, this was 'quite normal under the circumstances'. After a 'severe shock to the nervous system ... loss of memory proceeds nearly always on the same lines'. However, 'sooner or later' the memory would return, 'as suddenly as it went'. This might take 'a matter of months, sometimes it has been known to be as long as twenty years! Sometimes another shock does the trick. One restores what the other took away'.[3]

Shortly after the sinking of the *Lusitania*, Jane Finn adopted the name 'Janet Vandemeyer'. But when she subsequently sustained 'slight injuries to the head... in a street accident',[4] and recovered consciousness, she reverted to her true name. As Sir James had predicted, it was this second shock which enabled her to recover her memory.

Why did Jane Finn choose to assume the name 'Janet Vandemeyer'? This was because, after the sinking of the *Lusitania*, a Mrs Vandemeyer 'who had been very keen to look after me, and chum up with me generally' and her associates had knocked her unconscious. What could Jane now do to avoid them torturing her in order to make her reveal the whereabouts of the secret papers?

> Suddenly something put the thought of loss of memory into my head. The subject had always interested me, and I had read an awful lot about it. I had the whole thing at my finger-tips. If only I could succeed in carrying the bluff through, it might save me.[5]

I think I almost hypnotised myself. After a while, I almost forgot that I was really Jane Finn. I was so bent on playing the part of Janet Vandemeyer that my nerves began to play me tricks. I became really ill—for months I sank into a sort of stupor. I felt sure I should die soon, and that nothing really mattered.[6]

She was then examined by a doctor who 'experimented with various treatments'.[7]

In *The Secret Adversary*, Agatha described both how a shock to the nervous system caused amnesia in Jane Finn, and, on the other hand, how Jane feigned amnesia in order to escape from a dangerous and desperate situation.

The Disappearance of Mr Davenheim (1923)

For the last three days the papers have been full of the strange disappearance of Mr Davenheim, senior partner of Davenheim and Salmon, the well-known bankers and financiers. On Saturday he had walked out of his house, and had never been seen since. I should have thought that it would be almost impossible for anyone to 'disappear' nowadays.[8]

So said Captain Arthur Hastings, friend and associate of the great detective Hercule Poirot, in Agatha's novel *The Disappearance of Mr Davenheim*; published in 1923, three years prior to Agatha's own disappearance. Having considered the matter, Poirot now described how disappearances:

fall into 3 categories: First, and most common, the voluntary disappearance. Second, the much abused 'loss of memory' case—rare, but occasionally genuine. Third, murder and a more or less successful disposal of the body.[9]

This is reminiscent of Agatha's husband Archie discussing his wife's disappearance in his interview with the press.

To this, Hastings replied, 'You might lose your own memory, but someone will be sure to recognise you—especially in the case of a well-known man like Davenheim.' Furthermore, 'the domestic defaulter, is bound to be run down in these days of wireless telegraphy', and his 'appearance will be well known to everyone who reads a daily newspaper'.[10]

Poirot disagreed, and ventured the opinion that that the person who wilfully disappeared:

might bring intelligence, talent, a careful calculation of detail to the task; and then I do not see why he should not be successful in baffling the police force.[11]

Does this not suggest that three years before her own 'disappearance' in 1926, Agatha, who had been married to Archie for eleven years, was mulling over in her mind the possibility that she too might one day 'disappear'?

The Edge (1923)

In 1923, two years before Archie commenced his affair with Nancy Neele, Agatha described, in *The Edge*, how fury and indignation could be caused in one woman by the infidelity of another.

Gerald Lee became infatuated with the beautiful Vivien née Harper, and went on to marry her. However, when Clare Halliwell, who had a 'secret love' for Gerald, discovered that Vivien had been unfaithful to her husband with one Cyril Brown, she declared, 'I could ruin that woman'.[12] Clare now threatened to inform Gerald, unless Vivien confessed the matter to her husband. This Vivien could not do because she did not wish to 'have Cyril brought into it and ruined'.[13] She therefore threw herself over a cliff.

Giant's Bread (1930)

In Agatha's novel *Giant's Bread*, published in 1930 under the pseudonym Mary Westmacott, Vernon Deyre made a suicide attempt. Said he:

> There was a whacking great lorry coming down the road. I saw my chance—end it all—get out of it. I stepped out in front of it.

Deyre was hit, and rendered unconscious.

> When I came to, there was just one name in my head—George. That lucky chap, George. George Green.[14]

In other words, Deyre had undergone a change of identity. Furthermore, he now failed to recognize his wife Nell, and mistook his mistress, Jane, for his sister and his neighbour, Sebastian, for his brother.[15] He subsequently underwent 'treatment from a specialist' when, 'under hypnosis, part of the lost memory' returned.[16]

Surely, when Agatha wrote this novel, the memory of her car crash four years previously, at Newlands Corner, was still fresh in her mind, with all its unanswered questions. Like Deyre she: a) experienced amnesia; b) underwent a change of identity; c) failed to recognize her nearest and dearest; d) subsequently had treatment from a specialist, including hypnosis, and e) finally regained her memory, but not completely.

Harlequin's Lane (1930)

Mr Harley Quin and Mr Satterthwaite found themselves staying at 'Ashmead', Harlequin's Lane—otherwise known as 'Lovers' Lane'—the home of Anna and John Denham. As they were out walking together, Quin told Satterthwaite that the lane along which they were walking, belonged to him.

> They came round the last bend. The lane ended in a piece of waste ground, and almost at their feet a great pit opened.

This, it transpired, was a 'rubbish heap'.[17]

Quin overheard a conversation between John Denman and local resident Molly Stanwell. 'I can't live without you. What are we to do?' said Denman, his voice 'hoarse and anguished'.[18]

Satterthwaite guessed that Denman's wife Anna was, in fact, Anna Kharsanova, the great Russian dancer.[19] Russian prince Sergius Oranoff arrived to perform in a ballet, and he and Anna, whom he once knew and loved, met again after ten years.

When Anna goes missing the prince and Satterthwaite hurry to 'the deep pit', where they find 'something lying in it that had not been there before—the body of a woman ...'. It is she. Whereupon Oranoff weeps and says, 'I loved her. Always I loved her.'[20]

'A Lovers' Lane,' murmured Mr Satterthwaite, 'And people pass along it. And at the end of it—what do they find?'. Mr Quin smiled. He pointed at the ruined cottage above them. 'The house of their dreams— or a rubbish heap—who shall say?'[21]

In this sad and poignant story, is this not Agatha, reminiscing yet again about Newlands Corner and its chalk pit where, in a manner of speaking, all her hopes and dreams ended?

CHAPTER 20

Agatha's Disappearance, as Seen in a New Light

Agatha was an extremely ingenious person. So cleverly are her novels crafted, that they are usually impossible to solve, even despite the clues provided. However, although duplicity is to be expected in her fictional villains, to imagine Agatha (whose sense of what is right and what is wrong shines out, both in her novels and in her private life) to be equally dishonest, for example, by carrying out a monumental deception on her family, friends, and the public at large, is stretching credulity too far.

An intensely shy person, who loathed being in the limelight, the thought of herself being the subject of a nationwide manhunt, with the press swarming around her house and family and her photograph plastered over the front pages of the newspapers, would have been absolutely anathema to her.

As for Rosalind, it is equally impossible to conceive of Agatha being so cruel and hurtful as to a) fake her own suicide and b) pretend not to recognize her daughter when the two of them were reunited.

Evidence has been put forward that Agatha's suicide attempt was quite genuine. But how can her behaviour following the car crash be explained?

When, in the mid-1970s, half a century or so after Agatha's disappearance, Gwen Robyns discussed the matter of her disappearance with Dr Anthony Storr, Clinical Lecturer in Psychiatry at Oxford University, Storr expressed the opinion that Agatha was suffering from 'hysterical [now known as 'psychogenic' or 'dissociative] fugue'—the word fugue meaning 'flight from'. Said he:

> It is a well-recognised condition in people under great strain or tension. It is escaping from the mental as well as the physical pain of a situation if things have become intolerable.
>
> I think the fact that she took on the identity of the (i.e. Archie's) mistress is interesting. Here is a hated person—a person she must have resented passionately—and yet she puts herself in her shoes. In her disturbed state she may well have thought, 'How can I be like her to get my husband's affection back. How can I put myself in her shoes?' Something of that kind must have been going on in her mind.[1]

Although Storr took pains to describe hysterical fugue to Gwen Robyns,[2] the latter appears to have discounted this as a possibility, saying:

> As a woman of many years' experience, and having researched the entire episode for many months, I am of the opinion that Mrs Agatha Christie knew exactly what she was doing.
>
> Mentally distraught, filled with revenge, and in the degradation of her misery, she did just what many other women would have also done. She decided to teach her husband a lesson[3] [and having done so] she had only one recourse, and that was to sit tight until she was found and stick to her story of amnesia.[4]

Revenge on her errant husband may well have been Agatha's motive, but in respect of her time spent at the Harrogate Hydro, is Storr's opinion to be dismissed so easily?

Dissociative Fugue

'Dissociation' is defined by US psychiatrist Arnold M. Ludwig, as:

> A process whereby certain mental functions which are ordinarily integrated with other functions presumably operate in a more compartmentalised or automatic way, usually outside the sphere of conscious awareness or memory recall.[5]

In other words, in a fugue state, the human brain cannot visualise the picture as a whole.

In 1999, US psychiatrist Philip M. Coons, published the results of a study of five cases of 'Psychogenic or Dissociative Fugue'. This, said he:

> is a rare and little understood dissociative disorder … characterised by amnesia coupled with sudden unexpected travel away from one's home or place of work. One of the most remarkable findings in dissociative fugue is the propensity of individuals to travel long distances, usually without attracting attention to themselves. There is confusion about identity and sometimes new identity formation, either partial or complete.[6]
>
> The incidence of dissociative fugue increases during stressful events … Most dissociative fugues occur during the second through fourth decades of life. Although autobiographical memory is severely affected during dissociative fugue, procedural memories survive intact.

Therefore, when a person is in a state of fugue, he or she is quite capable of carrying out the procedures necessary for the pursuance of a seemingly normal life, as Agatha did during her time at Harrogate.

> Onset is abrupt and most dissociative fugues continue for a few days to a few weeks. Travel may take the individual hundreds of miles. Dissociative fugues may end either abruptly or gradually with persistent confusion or amnesia about identity.

Of the subjects who were evaluated in this study:

> the characteristics of the fugue states included amnesia, abrupt onset, trance-like state or perplexity, and partial new identity formation. Duration of the fugues was a mean of twenty-one days (range, 5-42 days). Cessation of the fugue was abrupt in two individuals and more gradual in three. Other psychiatric symptoms included depression … Possible aetiological factors included severe marital difficulties … Other psychiatric symptoms included depression.[7]

The *Diagnostic and Statistical Manual of Mental Disorders*, published by the American Psychiatric Association, states as follows:

During a fugue, individuals may appear to be without psychopathology [underlying mental disorder] and generally do not attract attention. Once the individual returns to the pre-fugue state, there may be no memory for the events that occurred during the fugue.

Such was the case with Agatha.

If a new identity is assumed during a fugue, it is usually characterised by more gregarious and uninhibited traits than characterized the former identity.

To wit, Agatha at The Hydro, singing, dancing, and playing the pianoforte.

The person may assume a new name, take up a new residence, and engage in complex social activities that are well integrated and that do not suggest the presence of a mental disorder. The onset of dissociative fugue is usually related to traumatic, stressful, or overwhelming life events.[8]
After return to the pre-fugue state, amnesia for traumatic events in the person's past may be noted.

This is of crucial importance, because if it was the case that Agatha had entered into a state of dissociative fugue, then this would explain why she developed longstanding amnesia.

Depression, dysphoria ['a state of unease, or general dissatisfaction with life'],[9] anxiety, grief, shame, guilt, psychological stress, conflict, and suicidal and aggressive impulses may be present.[10]

Both Agatha, and 'Celia' (in *Unfinished Portrait*), suffered from a number, if not all of the adverse symptoms mentioned above.

Although the concept of dissociation had been described earlier, for example by US physician Benjamin Rush (1745–1813), and by French psychiatrist Jacques-Joseph Moreau (1804–1884), it was French psychologist, philosopher, and psychotherapist Pierre Janet, who:

was the first to show clearly and systematically how it is the most direct psychological defense against overwhelming traumatic experiences. He demonstrated that dissociative phenomena play an important role in widely divergent post-traumatic stress responses which he included under the 19th-century diagnosis of hysteria.[11]

In other words, dissociation is a defence mechanism, which acts to protect a person from the effects of otherwise unbearable stress.

According to Professor of Philosophy Ian Hacking, the 'the first fuguer' to be described was (Jean-) Albert Dadas, born in 1860, a gas fitter from Bordeaux, who:

became notorious for his extraordinary expeditions to Algeria, Moscow, Constantinople. He travelled obsessively, bewitched, often without identity papers and sometimes without identity, not knowing who he was or why he travelled, and knowing only where he was going next. When he 'came to' he had little recollection of where he had been, but under hypnosis he would recall lost weekends or lost years.[12]

Medical student Philippe Tissié (1852–1935), who encountered Dadas in 1886, described his condition in a thesis entitled 'Les Aliénés Voyageurs' ('The Insane Travellers', 1887).[13] Fugue now 'became a medical disorder in its own right …'.[14] Since then, although fugue is a rare condition, cases of it have been reported on from all over the world.

In 1903, German Professor of Psychiatry, Karl Heilbronner, published a study of fifty-one cases of fugue, of which twenty were associated with epilepsy.[15] However, as far as is known, Agatha did not suffer from epilepsy.

In 1933, US psychiatrist Lloyd H. Ziegler, described three cases of fugue, and declared that 'the outstanding features in the history of these patients were personal problems of considerable magnitude'.[16]

To summarise, it is quite possible that the stress which Agatha was under at the time in question, was sufficient to induce in her a fugue state. However, when precisely she entered into this fugue state will be discussed shortly.

In normal circumstances, there is no doubt that Agatha would have contacted Carlo on the Saturday morning, as she had promised, to let her know her whereabouts, knowing that her secretary, who cared for her deeply, would be worried out of her mind. And Carlo would no doubt have reassured Rosalind that her mother was safe and well, and vice versa. In her fugue state, however, the names 'Carlo' and 'Rosalind' would have meant nothing to Agatha, extraordinary as this may seem.

Agatha's fugue state may also explain why, having arrived in London, where she would have had access to a telephone, she: a) failed to report the car crash to the police; b) made no arrangements to have her precious Morris recovered, and: c) failed to inform Carlo of her whereabouts and intentions, having promised so to do.

As a 'fuguer', Agatha's principal objective would have been to put a great deal of distance between herself and her normal place of residence. (This is perhaps why she opted to travel to the North of England, when there were other spas to choose from: at Bath, for example, which was only eighty miles from her home at Sunningdale, and therefore within easier reach.) So when she saw the poster at Waterloo Station advertising Harrogate, this would have been an attractive proposition to her: a) as a 'fuguer', because it was far removed from her home and: b) as a sufferer from neuritis, because there she could obtain expert treatment for her condition.

The adoption by Agatha of an assumed name—'Mrs Teresa Neele'—and a new identity is typical of a 'fuguer'. Furthermore, she placed her advertisement in *The Times* newspaper *under that name because, in her mind, she had become that person.*

Had she been in her normal frame of mind, Agatha, having learned of the furore which her disappearance had caused, and of the national manhunt—or to be more correct 'womanhunt'— which was now underway, would surely have felt it her duty, as a responsible citizen, to come forward immediately, however angry she was with her husband Archie. (And the same might be said of Nan Kon, if, as suggested by the Gardners, she had been privy to Agatha's plans, which is possible, but by no means certain.) However, as 'Mrs Neele', Agatha would not have recognized her own picture in the newspapers, nor identified with any of the personal details about herself given therein. She would, therefore, have had no reason to speak up.

For the same reason, Agatha failed to identify correctly either her husband Archie or the photograph of Rosalind, and, subsequently, Rosalind herself, when she was reunited with her daughter, for it was said that:

she [Rosalind] recalled going with her governess [Carlo] to her aunt's home in Cheshire, Abney Hall, where her mother went to stay after she was found, and finding that 'she did not remember anything we had been doing together or even the stories she used to tell me'.[17]

It is therefore not surprising that both Dr Wilson and Dr Core regarded Agatha's loss of memory as 'unquestionably genuine' (even though they failed to diagnose its cause—i.e. that she had entered a fugue state), and so, by all accounts, did Archie.

Agatha's behaviour during the time she was 'Mrs Neele' is therefore explicable in terms of her having entered a fugue state. However, this fact was evidently never explained to her, presumably because of ignorance on the part of her medical attendants, who failed to recognize it for what it was, and its aftermath left her in a state of permanent perplexity: one from which she never completely recovered.

In Agatha's novel *The Secret Adversary*, the heroine 'Jane Finn', appears to be on the verge of entering into a dissociative fugue state. Did Agatha herself have a propensity to this condition? After all, 'Dissociative Fugue … may be recurrent',[18] and therefore 'fuguers' often experience more than one episode of this disorder. However, there is no evidence that this was the case with Agatha.

In *Agatha Christie and the Eleven Missing Days*, Jared Cade made no mention of fugue, or dissociative state, let alone considered the possibility that this could a) have applied to Agatha, and b) account for her symptoms.

CHAPTER 21

Agatha's Continuing Perplexity

Janet Morgan, referring to Agatha's disappearance in December 1926, stated that:

> for many years, Agatha was worried by her failure completely to reconstruct the events of that dreadful time. After the [Second World] War she visited the Regius Professor of Pastoral Theology at Oxford, a well-known psychoanalyst, who did not practice professionally but regarded it as part of his university duties to help people who approached him voluntarily.[1]
>
> The information about Agatha Christie's consulting the Regius Professor came from a letter that Agatha's companion/secretary wrote some time after the fugue for Rosalind, Agatha's daughter to read when she was older.[2]

To which of Oxford's Regius professors did these statements refer? The most likely candidate is Robert Cecil Mortimer (1902–1976) who was Regius Professor of Pastoral Theology at Oxford University from 1945 to 1948. A notable author, his books include *The Elements of Moral Theology* (1947) and *Christian Ethics (1950). Professor Mortimer's daughter Sophia Schutts, confirms that her father and Agatha were indeed acquainted:*

> I remember him going to visit her in Devon to ask her to donate money for something [i.e. some charity] and she gave him the royalties of a short story. I do not think he had met her before then. This was in the [nineteen] fifties I think.[3]

Professor Mortimer, continued Janet:

> is said to have told Agatha that her experience had been extremely serious and, though he was unable to help her replace those missing hours, he tried to help her overcome her self-reproach.[4]

CHAPTER 22

Résumé

How fitting it is that Agatha Christie, the great crime novelist, has left her greatest mystery behind her for others to mull over and attempt to solve, after her death! The question is, can any sense be made of the episode of Agatha's disappearance in December 1926, or in other words, can the case be solved?

Anyone attempting to discover the entire truth about what happened prior to, during, and subsequent to the event is confronted with several obstacles. Eight decades have passed and, of its four major chroniclers, only one has included a bibliography, and only one has included any identifiable references in their works. Fortunately, however, a handful of important pieces of evidence survive. For example, Superintendent Kenward's report to the Home Office, dated 9 February 1927.

Other than that, the diligent researcher is obliged to rely upon press reports, and the uncorroborated reports of interviews conducted and statements made by the aforementioned biographers, and others who claimed to have knowledge of the event in question. This is in no way to imply that these biographers were not telling the truth, but rather to question whether some of the stated 'facts' may be relied upon, particularly those which have been passed down from generation to generation, or those which are hearsay.

It is often the case, in regard to the material relating to Agatha's disappearance, that there are discrepancies in respect of the 'facts' presented, or of the emphasis placed on the importance of these 'facts', depending on which particular source is consulted. Nevertheless, despite these caveats, it is possible to arrive at conclusions, based on the balance of probability, as to what really happened, and why, all those years ago.

By late 1926, Agatha had become convinced that she needed to leave home, for the sake of her own sanity, and on the evening of 3 December, she decided to make her getaway. First, however, she wrote three letters, which she left behind: one to Archie, one to Carlo, and another to Carlo which was only to be opened in the event of her death. But she omitted, in any of these letters (including the one to Archie, as far as is known), to give any information about her proposed destination. Before departing from Styles, she also composed a letter to her brother-in-law Campbell Christie, informing him that she intended to visit a Yorkshire spa. This, she proposed to post the following day to his place of work, in anticipation that it would be delivered to him on the Monday morning, by which time she would have made good her escape. Why did she disclose her true intentions to Campbell, but not to Carlo or to Archie? Presumably: a) because she did not wish her husband immediately to pursue her to Yorkshire, but preferred rather to keep him guessing for a while and: b) to have the comfort of knowing that she had done her duty by informing a member of the family of her whereabouts—though not precisely—lest the family should think that she had vanished from the face of the Earth.

At 10 o'clock that evening, having packed her belongings in her motor car, she set off —not for Yorkshire, but first for London (including Euston Station), and then Maidenhead and Sunningdale. The fact that she visited all these places, for no apparent reason, indicates that her mind was in turmoil. Finally, she arrived at Newlands Corner.

Admittedly, Agatha was depressed, which, in the circumstances in which she found herself, was hardly surprising, but was she so depressed as to make a suicide attempt? Janet Morgan thought not: 'Agatha was in despair but it would be wrong to imagine that she ever seriously contemplated suicide', she declared.[1] Both Archie and Superintendent Goddard, it will be recalled, were of the same opinion, as was Laura Thompson.

But Agatha, by her own account, gave the distinct impression that at the end of her long, night-time motor car journey, she *had* made a suicide attempt at Newlands Corner. Furthermore, her letter to Superintendent Kenward, a senior police officer, suggests that she had it in mind to stage some seemingly dramatic event in the county for which Kenward was responsible—i.e. Surrey, in which Newlands Corner was situated. The fact that Agatha's letter to Kenward was posted on the Friday night, indicates that she had decided on this course of action even before she left Styles. Why, therefore, did Agatha first drive from Styles to London, etc.? The probable answer is that two possibilities were passing through her mind at the same time: a) to travel to Yorkshire (her car had a range of 210 miles or so, on full tanks—main plus auxiliary—of petrol, so she could have accomplished the journey without the necessity of having to refuel *en route*), or: b) to take her own life.

Would it not have been simpler for Agatha to have made her getaway from Styles simply by walking, or taking a taxi to Sunningdale Station, from where she could have caught a train to London? Certainly, there was a train from Sunningdale at 10.57 p.m., arriving at London Waterloo at 12.05 a.m. However, the King's Cross to Harrogate train did not depart until 4.45 a.m.[2] This would therefore have been inconvenient, to say the least.

How was it that Agatha's car, when it was discovered, was found to contain personal possessions such as her dressing case, spare pairs of shoes, fur coat, etc.? This, presumably, was because she had packed in preparation for her visit to Harrogate.

Janet Morgan stated that, at Waterloo Station, Agatha 'saw a poster advertising the spa at Harrogate'. However, in view of her letter to Campbell, it is likely that this simply reinforced what was already in her mind—i.e. to visit that resort.

Agatha's critics

Agatha has been accused of pre-planning the entire operation—i.e. abandoning her car at Newlands Corner out of spite towards her unfaithful husband, and in order to cause him maximum embarrassment. To quote from the poet William Congreve:

> Heav'n has no rage, like love to hatred turn'd,
> Nor Hell a fury, like a woman scorn'd.[3]

Her actions, it is said, were also designed to elicit the maximum amount of sympathy and publicity for herself as an author. She has also been accused of feigning amnesia during and after her time spent at Harrogate. And she has been vilified both for failing to own up to what she had done, and for failing to apologize for the above misdemeanours.

Agatha in a fugue state

A significant reason why Agatha has been disbelieved in many quarters, in respect of her disappearance, is that insufficient attention has been paid to the possibility that she had entered a fugue state. But if it was the case that she had become a 'fuguer', precisely when did this transformation occur?

Agatha stated, in respect of the car crash, 'Up to this moment I was Mrs Christie. I knew I was Mrs Christie.'[4] This implies that after the car crash she did *not* know that she was Mrs Christie, presumably because she had entered into the fugue state. Had the blow on the head which Agatha sustained induced the fugue state? No, because fugue states are induced by stress and not by traumatic injuries to the head.

Agatha's amnesia

As Janet Morgan pointed out, even after many years, Agatha had still not been able to reconstruct in her mind 'the events of that dreadful time', and it:

> is virtually certain that her chronic amnesia was a consequence of the fugue state, rather than of a head injury sustained in the crash.

All is now explained

One of the most puzzling aspects of the crash and its aftermath is, why did Agatha leave her attaché case, her driving licence, and above all her fur coat behind, when she set out on a cold night for Clandon Station? Because, in her fugue state, she would not have recognized any of these items as belonging to her.

Supposing for instance, that when she arrived in London, Agatha had already entered into a fugue state. This would explain why: a), she failed to report the car crash to the police, and: b), why she made no arrangements for the recovery of her precious Morris Cowley. However, it was in London early that Saturday morning that she posted her letter to Campbell. As this letter was 'addressed from Styles', the conclusion must be that she took it to London with her, presumably having already stamped and addressed the envelope.

As already mentioned, in 'fuguers', 'procedural memories survive intact',[5] and it would therefore have been quite natural for Agatha to have posted the letter, even though, in her fugue state, the name Campbell Christie would in consequence have meant nothing to her.

Agatha's estimated time of arrival at London's Waterloo Station is between 8.25 a.m. and 9.01 a.m. on the morning of Saturday 4 December. So why did she opt to travel on the 1.40 p.m. train from King's Cross, when she could have caught an earlier one—say at 10.10 a.m. or 11.30 a.m.?[6] It is known that she went shopping and, according to Laura Thompson, that she visited Harrods, where she gave her name as 'Mrs Neele'.[7] In other words, she had, as a 'fuguer', now assumed the identity of Teresa Neele.

Although, as indicated earlier, Cade, based on what he was told by the Gardners, suggested that Agatha stayed the night of Friday 3 December with Nan Kon, the evidence does not support this. As for his suggestion that she met with Nan on the Saturday morning, the time scale would certainly have allowed for this. But if this was the case, then surely Nan would have noticed the change in Agatha's behaviour—and in particular that Agatha was now calling herself 'Mrs Neele', and raised the alarm. Furthermore, the fact that Nan evidently did not come forward with any evidence to assist the police with their enquiries, indicates that she had no information to give, and was just as much in the dark about Agatha and her movements as they were.

Other aspects of Agatha's behaviour, which were previously puzzling and seemingly inexplicable, may also be explained by her fugue state: her choice of an assumed name; her failure to recognize either her own photograph, or the account of her disappearance in the newspaper; or to realize that she was the cause of a nationwide 'manhunt'. It also explains: a) why she failed, at first, to recognize either her husband or her daughter, when they reappeared; b), why she never owned up to feigning amnesia (because she had not actually done so), and: c) why, for the remainder of her life, she was unable to recall full details of those lost eleven days. As for the placing by her of the advertisement in *The Times*, requesting that 'Teresa Neele's' friends or relatives come to visit her, this was not the action of a person in their right mind, but rather that of a 'fuguer', who believes themselves to be somebody else.

Finally, it explains why she never owned up to all those transgressions of which she was falsely accused, i.e. playing a foolish hoax on the police; attempting to teach her husband Archie a lesson, and even framing him for murder; deliberately adopting a false identity; and feigning amnesia.

Some criticisms addressed

Those who have chosen to criticise Agatha's account of her behaviour during this traumatic time in her life have failed to consider the possibility that she was telling the truth, at least as far as her fugue state, and the amnesia that was induced by it, permitted. This has led, not only to a great deal of confusion, but also to opprobrium being heaped upon Agatha by critics who lack the medical knowledge and expertise required to understand her condition.

For example, Gwen Robyns portrayed Agatha as being both spiteful and dishonest.

> I am of the opinion that Mrs Christie knew exactly what she was doing. Mentally distraught, filled with revenge, and in the degradation of her misery, she just did what many other women would have done. She decided to teach her husband a lesson. [And] once the powerful press got hold of the story … she had only one recourse and that was to sit tight until she was found and stick to her story of amnesia.[8]

Laura Thompson also implied that Agatha had not told the truth:

> It is said that she drove around for much of the night [in fact, Agatha herself said this], so distraught that she did not know where she was going. Yet two gallons of petrol were left in her car, so she cannot have driven very far.[9]

In fact, the capacity of the main and spare fuel tanks combined was more than adequate for a journey of that distance, as has already been demonstrated.

> It was said that Agatha did not recognise her daughter when she saw her again at Abney. This is impossible to believe, although it is very easy to imagine Agatha pretending to do such a thing.[10]

Such remarks indicate that Laura had not considered the possibility that Agatha had entered into a fugue state.

Jared Cade spoke of Agatha's 'fictionalized account of her movements on the night of her disappearance':[11]

> What Agatha's explanation did not take into account is that one cannot suffer from loss of memory and secondary personality at the same time. Medical experts are united on this.[12]

In fact, medical evidence points to the fact that, in a dissociative fugue state, with its concomitant amnesia, this is *exactly* what the 'fuguer' experiences.

Referring to Agatha's time spent at the Harrogate Hydro, Cade, who was evidently not acquainted with the phenomenon of dissociative fugue, declared:

> Of course a person with amnesia would have no difficulty in recognising her true identity on seeing herself in the newspapers.[13] [Agatha's] actions are the hallmarks of someone who has assumed a secondary personality or, alternatively, fashioned a new identity for an ulterior motive.[14]

Janet Morgan stated that 'Agatha was in despair but it would be wrong to assume that she ever seriously contemplated suicide.'[15] However, the evidence indicates not only that she contemplated suicide, but that she also went so far as to attempt it.

Clearly, once it is accepted that Agatha was in a fugue state, than all these seeming contradictions are resolved.

In February 1928, Mitchell Hedges had claimed that Agatha had perpetrated a 'foolish hoax' on the police.[16] Quite the contrary. Her suicide attempt was a manifestation of the immense frustration, desperation, and hurt that she felt, as a result of her abandonment by Archie, for whom she still had deep feelings. And her disappearance, change of identity, and amnesia were manifestations of the fugue state which she had entered into and over which she had no control.

* * *

As is often the case with Agatha, details of her personal life found their way into her novels. For example, in *Why Didn't They Ask Evans*, published in 1934, Lady Frances Derwent ('Frankie') staged an 'accident' by crashing her motor car into a wall and pretending to be concussed. This was in order to gain access to Merroway Court, home of Henry and Sylvia Bassington-ffrench.[17]

Moira Nicholson, the doctor's wife, told Frankie's friend and accomplice, Bobby Jones, that she was 'terribly frightened. I'm afraid I'm going to be murdered'—i.e. by Dr Nicholson—she said.

Why? Because her husband wished to marry Sylvia, having disposed of the latter's husband Henry.[18] Roger Bassington-ffrench, brother of Henry, said of Moira, 'She probably believes quite honestly that he is trying to kill her—but is there any foundation in fact for that belief? There doesn't seem to be.'[19] Bobby, however, 'believed implicitly every word Moira had uttered. Her fears were neither the result of a vivid imagination nor yet of nerves'.[20] Bobby's faith in Moira was unjustified, for it transpired that Moira's story was a fabrication.

Was this, in reality, Agatha, on the one hand acknowledging to herself that, prior to her departure from Styles, she had feared that Archie was trying to poison her, while on the other, debating in her mind whether or not such fears were simply a figment of her imagination?

When Roger, disguised as Dr Nicholson, took Bobby and Frankie prisoner, she asked him 'What are you going to do with us?'. Roger told her that he intended to stage an 'accident', whereby:

> Lady Frances Derwent, driving her car, her chauffeur beside her, mistakes a turning and takes a disused road leading to a quarry. The car crashes over the edge. Lady Frances and her chauffeur are killed.[21]

In real life, Edward McAlister's statement that 'the woman drove the car very slowly away downhill towards Merrow' suggests that Agatha, on her approach to Newlands Corner that fateful night in December 1926, also mistook a turning—i.e., she turned right 100 yards or so too soon, off the A25, and found herself in Trodd's Lane. She then rectified her mistake, and turned into Water Lane, where the chalk pit was situated. Thankfully, however, Agatha did not crash over the edge.

Clearly, even in 1934, almost a decade after her disappearance, the memory of Newlands Corner was still very much in Agatha's mind.

* * *

In her 'Whodunnits', Agatha's objective was to disguise the identity of the villain until the very last moment, when he or she would finally be exposed and brought to justice. How paradoxical, therefore, that in regard to her disappearance in 1926, she herself was cast as the villain of the piece, when in fact, she was the victim!

CHAPTER 23

Latter Years

Not surprisingly, in 1928, the year of her divorce from Archie, only one work by Agatha was published—*The Big Four*. Her output subsequently picked up again, as follows: 1928, three; 1929, four; 1930, four. Between 1931 and 1976, the year of her death, the total was ninety-one, with another ten works being published posthumously. Favourite themes in her novels were the locations in South Devonshire where she had spent her childhood, including Torquay, Burgh Island, and Dartmoor; aeroplanes, golf, pets, and steam trains.

When, in the autumn of 1928, Agatha was invited out to dinner with friends in London, a chance meeting with a young naval officer, Commander Howe, and his wife, changed her life forever. Agatha, who 'had always been faintly attracted to archaeology, though knowing nothing about it,' was already aware of the work of English archaeologist Leonard Woolley at Ur in Iraq. Now, having extolled the virtues of Baghdad, that country's capital city from where he had recently returned, the Commander suggested that she might like to journey there by train, in fact by the most famous train in the world—The Orient Express.

Soon, this idea of Howe's became a reality and, having travelled to Damascus, capital of Syria, where she spent three days, Agatha finally arrived at Ur, where she was welcomed by Woolley, and by his wife Katharine (who had recently read and enjoyed Agatha's *The Murder of Roger Ackroyd*, and was 'given the VIP treatment'. Katharine became one of Agatha's closest friends.[2]

Katharine arranged for Agatha to visit the Iraqi cities of Nejef (the Muslim holy city of the dead) and Kerbala, which had 'a wonderful mosque' with a gold and turquoise dome.[3] On her journey she was escorted by Max Mallowan, who for the last five years had been Woolley's assistant. There followed an expedition to view a crusader's castle at Kalaat Simon (Iraq).[4] At Mersin on the Turkish coast, which they also visited, Max and Agatha enjoyed a picnic and found themselves surrounded by a landscape awash with yellow marigolds, some of which he picked, made into a chain, and hung around her neck.[5] At this, Agatha, who loved flowers, would have been delighted. It was while they were swimming in the clear blue waters of a desert lake at Ukhaidir (Iraq), that Max decided that Agatha 'would make an excellent wife for him'.[6]

On hearing that her daughter Rosalind had contracted pneumonia, Agatha decided that she must travel home as quickly as possible. Max offered to travel with her. When Max proposed marriage, Agatha's instinct was to refuse him, on the grounds that: a) she was thirteen years his senior and b) he was a Roman Catholic, whereas she was an Anglican. Agatha confessed that re-marrying was the last thing on her mind. '*I must be safe*', she said; in other words, safe from anyone ever being able to hurt her again.[7] However, she did admit that she and Max shared a great many common interests, and that to her, his work as an archaeologist was far more fascinating than any of her former husband Archie's financial transactions in the City of London.[8] Another positive factor was that Rosalind clearly liked Max, and approved of him. Finally, on 11 September 1930, the couple were married in the chapel of St Columba's Church in Edinburgh. They spent their honeymoon in Venice, Yugoslavia and Greece.

A year previously, on 20 September 1929, Agatha's brother Monty, who was in Marseilles at the time, died unexpectedly of a cerebral haemorrhage whilst at a café on the sea front. He was interred in that city's military cemetery.[9]

The play *Alibi*, which made its debut in 1928, was the first to be produced from one of Agatha's books—*The Murder of Roger Ackroyd*. *Murder at the Vicarage*, published in 1930, was the first novel to feature Miss Jane Marple, described by Agatha as the kind of elderly lady whom she imagined would have resembled some of her grandmother's 'Ealing cronies'.[10] Whereas Hercule Poirot comes across as being sophisticated, fastidious, and dapper, Miss Marple contents herself with the simple pleasures of life—having a nice cup of tea, gardening, attending flower shows. Perhaps the altogether more relaxed environs in which Miss Marple operated, and the fact that she was female, made a welcome change for Agatha when it came to portraying the character of the female sleuth.

Agatha took a keen interest in the work of her husband Max, describing the years from 1930 to 1938, when he and she were excavating in Iraq and later in Syria, as 'particularly satisfying because they were so free of outside shadows'.[11] It became the couple's habit to leave England in December or January; travel to the Middle East, and return the following March, after a season's digging.

Max's next assignment was at Nineveh (Iraq), where Agatha joined him for a dig on the Quyunjik Mound—with the River Tigris just one mile away. When Max (now assistant to Reginald Campbell Thompson) discovered the remains of the potter's shop with splendid crockery, vases, and other 'polychrome pottery all shining in the sun', which had laid untouched for about 6,000 years, Agatha felt she was 'bursting with happiness'.[12] After a period spent at Arpachiyah (Iraq), Max moved in 1932, to Syria: first to Chagar Bazar, and in 1937 to Tell Brak. Meanwhile, in December 1934, the couple purchased an additional property 'Winterbrook House' at Wallingford in Oxfordshire. As for Agatha's daughter Rosalind; after leaving her girls' public school, Benenden, Kent, she spent time on the Continent and learnt to speak fluent French. On one occasion she joined Agatha and Max in Syria on a dig.

According to Janet Morgan, 'Rosalind got on well with her step-father ... She had adjusted well to the new situation'. As for Archie, 'Rosalind enjoyed her father's games and teasing and managed to remain staunchly loyal to both her parents'.[13]

The couple finally returned to England, to Number 48 Sheffield Terrace, London; another house which Agatha owned. In 1939, Agatha and Max added yet another to their portfolio of properties—'Greenway', Churston Ferrars, Devonshire. This was a Georgian mansion standing in extensive grounds, overlooking the River Dart, and dating from about 1780.

When the Second World War broke out in September 1939, Max joined the Home Guard at Brixton, Devon, and Agatha volunteered to work once again in the dispensary at the hospital in Torquay. Later, she joined Max in London, and Greenway was let for use as a nursery for children evacuated from the St Pancras district of London. The property was subsequently requisitioned by the Admiralty and taken over by officers of the United States Navy. In 1940, Rosalind married Hubert Prichard, a major in the regular army. From that year until 1945, Max served in the Royal Air Force Volunteer Reserve as Liaison Officer with Allied forces, and as Civilian Affairs Officer in North Africa.[14]

When 48 Sheffield Terrace was bombed, Agatha and Max moved to a flat in Hampstead. He was now working at the Air Ministry; she commenced work in the dispensary at University College Hospital. On 21 September 1943, Agatha's grandson Mathew Prichard was born. Agatha described the boy as a most rewarding person to be in company with, and it was his 'incurably optimistic temperament' which she found to be particularly attractive.[15] It was to Mathew that she bequeathed the play *The Mousetrap* (the stage version of *Three Blind Mice*, written to celebrate HM *Queen Mary*'s 80th birthday in 1947). There were many other beneficiaries of Agatha's books and stories, including family and friends, and also organizations, such as the Westminster Abbey Appeal Fund and her local church at Churston Ferrers, to which she donated a stained glass window.

In August 1944, Agatha's daughter Rosalind received a telegram to say that her husband, Hubert Prichard, had been killed in action in France. When the war ended in September 1945, Greenway was derequisitioned by the Admiralty.

In 1947, Max, now Professor of Western Asiatic Archaeology at London University, returned with Agatha to the Middle East after an absence of ten years. Here, as Director of Iraq's British School of Archaeology, he would organize a dig at Nimrud, once the military capital of Assyria—a project which would take twelve years. In this endeavour, Agatha, who was as enthusiastic as her husband, declared that she was unashamedly attached to the 'objects of craftsmanship and art' which were unearthed as the result of Max's archaeological digs. And most fascinating to her of all were those objects crafted by the labour of the human hand. This included 'the little pyxis [casket] of ivory with musicians and their instruments carved round it; the winged boy' and the bust of a woman's head, which to her eyes was 'ugly', yet 'full of energy and personality'.[16]

Referring to the excavations at Nimrud, which she admitted had been defaced by the archaeologists' bull-dozers, Agatha declared, confidently, that before long its scars would heal, and that the flowers that had previously grown there in early spring would do so once again.[17] In respect of the people of the Iraqi city of Mosul, she commented on how good it was to have friends such as these: 'Warm-hearted, simple, full of enjoyment of life', and with such a well-developed sense of humour. Whenever she happened to travel through a village where one of their workmen had his home, he would immediately rush out and offer hospitality, demanding that she and Max join him in a drink of sour milk. Absolutely devoted to this region of the world, she declared, 'I love it still and always shall.'[18] Meanwhile, in October 1948, Agatha's daughter Rosalind was remarried, to barrister Anthony Hicks.

And so, at last, Agatha had found that joy and contentment for which she had so long yearned; a yearning which she alluded to over and over again in her writing. For example, in *Triangle at Rhodes* (published in 1936), Marjorie Gold, in reference to herself and her husband Douglas, says to Hercule Poirot 'Well, one does feel very grateful for one's own happiness.'

Having spent a decade or more of winters in the Middle East it is hardly surprising that Agatha wrote many novels based on this region, and from her writings it is clear that its people and their customs became very dear to her heart. It was at the suggestion of Stephen Glanville (Professor of Egyptian Archaeology and Philology at University College, London, from 1935–1946), that Agatha wrote *Death Comes as the End* (published in 1945), a detective story set in Ancient Egypt.

In *Murder in Mesopotamia* (1936), Poirot, in an effort to discover who has murdered Louise, wife of archaeologist Dr Eric Leidner, assembled all the suspects together, as was his custom. He then began his address to them by quoting a phrase in Arabic: 'Bismillahi ar rahman ar rahim,' which he translated into English: 'In the name of Allah, the Merciful, the Compassionate.'[19] (Each and every chapter of the *Koran* begins with these words). There are references to ancient artefacts: an exquisite golden dagger, its handle set with precious stones, and an equally exquisite golden drinking-vessel, embossed with figures of the heads of rams. This cup, which was unique and dated from the Early Akkadian Period (Akkad—a northern Semitic people who conquered the Sumerians in 2350 BC and ruled Mesopotamia), was described as one of the most beautiful ever found anywhere in the world.[20] All these artefacts were excavated from the grave of a prince.

Murder on the Orient Express (1934) is centred, needless to say, on the train which took Agatha for her first visit to the Middle East, and on which she would travel many times subsequently. *Death on the Nile* (1937) is set aboard the steamer SS *Karnak*, as it embarks on a Nile cruise. *Come, Tell me how you Live* (1946), an autobiographical account of Agatha's life with Max at their archaeological camp headquarters in Syria, was given by Agatha as a present to Max on his return from the Second World War.

Of all the plays that Agatha wrote, she described *Witness for the Prosecution* (1948) as the one she liked best, and felt most satisfied with.[21] Despite her increasing success, however, the shyness that had been the bane of her life remained with her. Having attended the opening night, she crept away just as soon as the curtain had come down. It was to no avail, because members of the public caught sight of her. They surrounded her car, uttered words of encouragement and requested that she sign their autograph books. The effect of this warm welcome on Agatha was dramatic, and, just for once, she found that her 'self-consciousness and nervousness' had evaporated.[22] In 1956, HM Queen Elizabeth II appointed her Commander of the Most Excellent Order of the British Empire (CBE).

Archie's wife Nancy Christie (née Neele) died in August 1958. When, on 2 December 1959, Madge's sister-in-law and great friend Nan Kon died, Agatha was devastated. That year, Greenway was transferred by Agatha to her daughter Rosalind, who, together with her husband Anthony Hicks, took up residence there in 1968 and lived there until her death.[23]

On 20 December 1962, Agatha's first husband Archie died aged 73. That year, she was invited to attend a party to celebrate the tenth anniversary of the opening of her play *The Mousetrap*. It was to become the longest running play of all time.

In 1965, Agatha donated the sum of £310,000 to the Harrison Homes for Elderly Ladies of Limited Means (of which there were eighteen in the London suburbs of Kensington and Hammersmith). This was followed by further gifts totalling £50,000.[24]

When in 1968, Max was knighted, Agatha became Lady Mallowan. In 1971, her eightieth year, she was made Dame Commander of the Most Excellent Order of the British Empire (DBE).

Agatha Christie is the best-selling novelist of all time. In her lifetime, her published works included sixty-six crime novels, thirteen short story collections, six other novels, an autobiography, and fifteen plays. Her works have been translated into all the world's major languages, and many have been adapted for the cinema, television, radio, and for video games.

CHAPTER 24

Agatha's Enduring Popularity

Agatha's novels cry out 'Englishness!' at every turn, and, even abroad, her fictional English travellers endeavour to observe the customs of their native land. Meanwhile, in the home country, the vicar inhabits his vicarage; the squire—usually a retired army officer—his stately home; Miss Marple her idyllic cottage; and Poirot his London apartment. Traditions, such as church on Sunday, afternoon tea, and tennis on the lawn, are there to be observed, and etiquette and good manners a *sine qua non*, at least among the cognoscenti.

The class system exists, certainly, but at its most benign, so that the aristocracy and gentry almost invariably treat their servants with courtesy and kindness, and they in turn act with due deference and humility, to make a harmonious, if somewhat unrealistic, whole!

And yet times are changing. When, in *The Mirror Crack'd from Side to Side*, Mrs Dolly Bantry becomes a widow, she moves out of Gossington Hall and into the Lodge, having sold her former property to a film actress Marina Gregg, whereupon Marina installs a new, marble bathroom in the property, and Dolly discovers a washing machine in her new abode. Meanwhile, a new housing development springs up in Miss Marple's village of St Mary Mead, where one of the residents has purchased a motorcycle, which he rides furiously up and down the lanes.

The novels, of course, lend themselves to adaptations for cinema and television, when red telephone boxes, seaside piers, Punch and Judy shows, morris dancing, brass bands which entertain in the parks, the typical English garden with its herbaceous borders, the village 'bobby' on his bicycle, the alluring sports cars for which the country was famous, magnificent mansions replete with *Objet d'art*, fine furniture and paintings, all give an extra and colourful dimension to the proceedings.

Agatha's protagonists, the conservative Miss Jane Marple and the flamboyant Monsieur Hercule Poirot are strong and uncompromising in their search for truth and desire to see justice done and retribution delivered. As millionaire philanthropist and man of letters Jason Rafiel says in *Nemesis*, in a quotation from the biblical book of Amos: 'Let judgment run down as like waters, and righteousness as a mighty stream'.[1] Such sentiments would have chimed well with Agatha's readers who are given an insight into the privileged, and sometimes scandalous, life of lords and ladies, and squirearchy and gentry; to wealth, high finance, and exotic locations. For in her novels she invites the reader to journey with her, not only into the beautiful English countryside, but also to Europe, the USA, the Middle East, and the Caribbean.

Whether Agatha's genius as a storyteller was an inherent quality, or whether it was learned, is a matter for debate. However, there is no doubt that, as a child, her love of stories was nurtured principally by her mother Clara, her sister Madge, and 'Nursie'. Later, when Agatha taught herself to read, she said the whole 'world of story books was open to me', and 'I demanded books'.[2] And of these, there was a plentiful supply, not only at Ashfield, but at the home of 'Auntie-Grannie'.[3] Agatha was particularly fond of the Bible's Old Testament stories, in which she had 'revelled from an early age'.[4] When she was taught French, she was then able to read books in that language also.[5] Meanwhile, her taste for drama was nurtured by her weekly visits to the theatre in Torquay.[6]

When Agatha was 'lying in bed recovering from influenza' and her mother suggested that she wrote a story, Clara could never had imagined that her daughter would one day become the best-selling crime writer of all time![7] It was Madge (who herself had already had several short stories accepted by the magazine *Vanity Fair*),[8] who introduced Agatha to Sir Arthur Conan Doyle's famous detective, Sherlock Holmes, whereupon the two sisters became 'connoisseurs of the detective story'.[9] It was therefore no coincidence that Agatha's first published novel, *The Mysterious Affair at Styles*, should be a 'whodunnit'!

One of the many examples of Agatha's genius is *Murder on the Orient Express*, published in 1934. Poirot is returning from Syria on this famous train, when a murder is committed. Shortly afterwards the train comes to a halt in the Yugoslavian countryside, when it is trapped in a snowdrift.

As far as Poirot is concerned, there are thirteen suspects, all occupants of the carriage in question. They include British Army Officer Colonel Arbuthnot; Hungarian diplomat Count Andrenyi and his wife the Countess; Russian Princess Dragomiroff and her German maid; American former actress Mrs Hubbard and Swedish missionary Greta Ohlsson. To create such a scenario, in which each character interacts with all the others, and continues to do so as the plot progresses, was an accomplishment of consummate brilliance, comparable with that of a grand master playing a game of chess, or an orchestral composer creating a symphony.

But there was far more to Agatha than the ability to create a technically sound plot for her detective novels. Closeted as her early life may have been, she nevertheless became an avid student of human nature, and her ability to discover what motivated people and 'made them tick', comes through in the characters of her novels. For example, when her tutor, 'Mr P', the 'best-known pharmacist' in Torquay, admitted to Agatha that he was in the habit of carrying in his pocket 'a dark-coloured lump' of curare, the South American arrow poison, because it made him, 'feel powerful',[10] this gave his pupil an insight into the mind of a murderer—which is not to say that 'Mr P' himself would have considered murdering anybody, of course! Also, Agatha's own personal experiences of life—bereavement, financial difficulties, interpersonal relationship problems within her family, falling in love, divorce, and loneliness, for example, also enabled her to portray her characters in an authentic and credible manner. As Carla Lemarchant said to Poirot in *Five Little Pigs*, 'I've heard about you. The things you've done. The *way* you have done them. It's psychology that interests you, isn't it?'[11]

With Agatha, the reader knows that a detective novel by her always comes with a cast iron, yet unspoken guarantee: that the plot will be ingenious, the location interesting and often exotic; and the suspense maintained right the way through until the end. The narrative will be laced with tantalising clues, which are periodically dangled in front of the reader, challenging him or her to compete with Poirot, Miss Marple, Tommy and Tuppence Beresford, or Parker Pyne, to identify the murderer. What fun! But so clever was Agatha at spinning a web of intrigue that, for example in *The ABC Murders*, there seems to no doubt whatsoever that Alexander Cust is guilty, and yet this proves not to be the case!

Furthermore, her characters were strongly drawn and therefore memorable, both by name and by nature, as, for example, in *The Body in the Library*, which features Colonel and Mrs Bantry of Gossington Hall; the wealthy Conway Jefferson, all of whose family has been killed in an aeroplane crash; Conway's adopted daughter Ruby Keene, a professional dancer, and the young and flamboyant artist Basil Blake, discoverer of Ruby's dead body in the library at the hall.

The reader can expect to be frightened, but is always secure in the knowledge that Hercule Poirot or Miss Jane Marple will finally bring the murderer to justice. And the notion of justice is greatly appealing, for it is deeply embedded in the human psyche, and Agatha was well aware how a sense of injustice can lead to indignation—hatred even—and a desire for revenge and restitution on the part of the victim. So it is essential that virtues such as love, compassion, selflessness and self-sacrifice and honesty prevail against vices such as greed, gambling, jealousy, and infidelity, and Agatha laces her novels with numerous biblical quotations, extolling the virtues of righteousness, and issuing dire warnings to those who transgress!

Epilogue

Agatha Christie was a person to whom, as a child, home and all that went with it—i.e., her family, nannie, toys, pets and garden, were all important. The same was true of friends, although sadly, in her young life, she tended to be somewhat isolated from the outside world, as already described. These deep feelings of attachment made her particularly vulnerable to loss of any kind.

The importance to her of Ashfield, the family home in Torquay, is demonstrated by the fact that she hung on to it long after her mother's death when she could ill afford to do so, owing to the high cost of its maintenance and upkeep. Nonetheless, she had no regrets on this score: 'Though to hold on to it may have been foolish, it gave me something that I value, a treasure of remembrance.'[1] Subsequently, wherever she lived, Ashfield remained her idea of an ideal home.

When, in the early 1960s, Agatha learned that Ashfield was to be demolished and a new estate developed on the site, she decided, after an interval, to pluck up courage and drive up Barton Road. Here, to her horror, she discovered that in place of her former home, a new estate consisting of 'the meanest, shoddiest little houses' had been erected. The great trees, including the beech, the Wellingtonia, the pines, the elms, and the ilex, together with the ash trees in the wood had disappeared. All that remained was a stunted monkey-puzzle tree which was barely surviving in someone's backyard. There was no garden, let alone any grass to be seen. Everything had been asphalted over, and another link with the past had gone forever.[2]

Anything that threatened her safe, some might say cocooned, existence was therefore a source of anxiety: something which could even precipitate one of those night terrors from which she suffered as a child. The repeated bouts of ill health which afflicted both her parents, epitomised such a threat. When she was aged eleven, Agatha's father Frederick—'the rock upon which the home is set'[3]—died, after which she meandered around the house in a state of mental turmoil. This was indeed a calamity, something which she had never anticipated could happen.[4] When her mother Clara, suffered a series of 'bad heart attacks', Agatha described getting up at night, creeping along the corridor, kneeling down by her mother's bedroom door with her head to the hinge where a reassuring snore would comfort her. However, if no snoring was to be heard, she would remain at the door in a crouched position, feeling not only dejected, but intensely afraid.[5] When her beloved 'Nursie' retired, she described this as 'the first real sorrow of my life …'.[6] But there was a more sinister burden which she was also obliged to bear: that of The Gunman who always seemed to be lingering about, haunting her and threatening to disrupt the 'noiseless tenor' of her way.[7]

Repeatedly, both in her autobiography and her books, Agatha described how friends were so vitally important; particularly those of long standing. She was equally attached to her pet dogs, and to her canary Goldie, and was distraught when the latter flew away one day, describing it as 'the supreme catastrophe'.[8] When the creature reappeared alive, she cried tears of relief and joy.

When Agatha embarked on a world tour with husband Archie and Major E. A. Belcher, she described how travel 'brings occasional homesickness and loneliness, and pangs of longing' to be reunited with 'some dearly loved person—Rosalind, my mother, Madge'.[9]

From an early age, Agatha made it clear that her main ambition was to achieve a happy marriage and be part of a happy family—such as she had enjoyed as a child. When she met Archie, she truly believed that her dream of marital happiness had come true. When he demanded a divorce, this to her was an event of such cataclysmic proportions that it temporarily unhinged her mind; sending her into shock, and precipitating what today is called a 'dissociative fugue state'. At the time, the art of psychiatry being less advanced than it is now, nobody realised or accurately diagnosed the malady from which she was suffering (even though numerous examples of the condition had already been described). Nowadays, one would hope that she would have been treated more expertly, and with greater understanding and compassion.

'Celia', in *Unfinished Portrait*, voiced Agatha's thoughts when she declared that as a child, the balance of her life had been wrong: 'My home was too happy. It made me grow up a fool.' That is to say, Agatha's childhood had not prepared her for life in the real world beyond. This may have been a factor in her reaction to the stress caused by the breakdown of her marriage, when she felt that she could no longer cope, and subsequently—albeit temporarily—entered into a fugue state.

Agatha died on 12 January 1976 at 'Winterbrook' aged 85, having been married to Max for forty-five years. On that day, West End theatres dimmed their lights in her honour. She was buried at nearby Cholsey village. On 13 May a memorial service was held for her at London's St Martin-in-the-Fields. Her autobiography was published, posthumously, the following year.

Amongst her many belongings were discovered 'the attaché case that contained Archie's love letters, and the wedding ring he gave her'.[10] Surely, this speaks volumes about Agatha's enduring love for Archie, despite all.

In 1977 Max Mallowan was remarried to Barbara Parker, daughter of a Royal Naval Captain who had been his assistant in Iraq. He died on 19 August 1978 at Wallingford, Oxfordshire.

Rosalind died on 28 October 2004, aged 85.

Appendices

Appendix 1
Superintendent William Kenward

When Kenward joined the Surrey Constabulary, he was allocated the collar number '96' (which was later changed to number '47'). Prior to that, he had worked as a gardener.

In March 1900, Kenward, then aged twenty-five, was 'highly commended' by the Chief Constable for excellent detective work and courageous conduct in the licensed victualing cases at Haslemere and Puttenham. In July 1903 he was again commended, 'for ability and energy in the capture of Charles Vincent for burglary at Frimley', and in August 1909, 'for rendering First Aid to a man who had cut his throat'.

During the First World War (1914–1918), Kenward was a dog handler at Camberley Police Station. At that time bloodhounds were used to track German escapees from the prisoner of war camp established at Frith Hill, Frimley.[1] On 31 December 1921, he was awarded the King's Police Medal, having tackled and arrested a 'madman armed with a rifle at Woking who had already wounded a constable'.[2] The medal was bestowed upon him personally by His Majesty King George V on 27 June 1921.

In 1923, Kenward was criticized by *The Scotsman* newspaper for taking the view 'that it should be an offence to build a touring car which has a greater speed than thirty miles an hour'.[3] Some might say Kenward was taking a generous view, when the speed limit for the time was only 20 mph. Said Tom Roberts:

> When he was first appointed Superintendent at Godalming in 1921, divisional superintendents had no motor vehicle, but they were provided with a horse and trap to travel around their divisions. The following story was told to me by his groom who often travelled with him.
>
> Superintendent Kenward had not been at Godalming many months before the horse put on weight from the various tidbits he gave it on his frequent visits to the stable. As a result, when they were out driving, the horse would soon show signs of tiring and Mr Kenward would insist that he and the groom walk up the hills—which the groom found embarrassing and a little ridiculous, and the public amusing. When he became Deputy Chief Constable and moved into the heart of Guildford there were flocks of pigeons, usually referred to as town pigeons, which visited the Headquarters building daily, many of them looking thin and emaciated. At his own expense he bought corn, mostly maize, every week and these birds were fed in the yard of police headquarters by him or under his direction every day.[4]
>
> As I got to know Mr Kenward better I found him to be 'a man of great compassion; he would show this in many ways while doing his utmost to avoid publicity'.[5]

The brusque manner which he displayed appeared to be a part of the armour of most police officers. In Mr. Kenward's case it certainly belied the true character which lay beneath. He was a man who hated cruelty of any kind whether to humans, to animals or birds.[6]

In 1926, Kenward founded the General Fund for Widows and Orphans for the Surrey Constabulary.

Superintendent Kenward retired on 31 July 1931. He died on 14 May the following year. His conduct during his years of service would subsequently be described as exemplary after thirty-one years of approved service.[7] Said Tom Roberts:

He had been my Superintendent up till the date of his retirement except for those first few months of my service at Woking. Although I did not know him very well he struck me as a man of great ability and I regarded him very highly. Everything I saw of him in connection with the Police Service impressed me.[8]

On 3 October 2007, *The Times newspaper, referring to 'The Mysterious Episode in 1926', declared:*

Ponds were dragged and the surrounding countryside searched by Police and volunteers, because bungling Superintendent Kenward of the Surrey Constabulary was convinced that Archie had murdered his wife.

In all the circumstances, this appears to be an unfair criticism of a diligent and devoted police officer.

Appendix 2
Tom Roberts

Having served with the Surrey Constabulary from 1926 until 1953, Tom Roberts worked for the security services, and following that, as an Industrial Security Advisor to various large corporations and industrial companies.

Appendix 3
Superintendent Charles Goddard

From 1901, when he was aged forty, Goddard served as Inspector at Wokingham (the headquarters of the Berkshire County Police being situated at Reading), and from 1903 as Superintendent in charge of the Wokingham Division.[1]

In the early days, transportation for police officers was by horse, bicycle or train, but, in 1919, six motor cars were supplied to the Berkshire Constabulary by the Ford Motor Company, at a cost of £275 each (together with three horses at £70 each).[2] At Wokingham, Superintendent Goddard:

was particularly keen on drill. Many men can still recall with … a certain amount of pride, the days when they were stationed at Wokingham and formed part of a line of men paraded across the road and then 'doubled' to the Town Hall to surround that edifice with all possible speed. This drill proved to the Superintendent that his men could be dispatched to a given point in the shortest possible time, or alternatively, deal with 'a truculent mob'.[3]

Superintendent Goddard retired from the Wokingham Division in November 1932, after fifty-one years' service.

Appendix 4
Harrogate Spa

It is interesting to digress for a moment and consider how Harrogate's reputation as a spa town came about, and also why a visit to Harrogate Spa would have been such an attractive proposition to someone like Agatha, who suffered from severe and chronic neuritis.

It was in 1571 that William Slingsby of Bilton Park discovered that cold spring water from a natural well at Stray Common, Harrogate, had health-giving properties similar to that of spa waters in Belgium. He named this the 'Tewit Well', after a resident bird, the peewit (or lapwing). In 1631, a second well was discovered nearby, by Michael Stanhope. Travellers were now attracted to the town, and by 1660, 'Harrogate Spa' as the town came to be called, had rapidly expanded. In 1663 the first public bathing house was built, and by the end of the century there were twenty such houses. By 1770 it was said that Harrogate was well established as a spa town and doctors produced leaflets about the quality of the water.

Altogether, eighty-eight cold springs were discovered: thirty-six in the valley gardens, less than half a mile from the Old Swan Hotel, where Jonathan Shutt began to receive visitors at the 'Sign of the Swan'—later known as The Swan Inn, and finally, in 1840, as the Old Swan Hotel. In that year, the first railway terminus was built in Harrogate, enabling more visitors to access the town.

In 1842 it was stated that Isaac Thomas Shutt was the last of the Shutts to own the Old Swan Hotel. He was a trained architect and surveyor, whose plans were used for the design of the new Royal Pump Rooms, built to house 'the old sulphur well'—otherwise known as 'The Stinking Well', for obvious reasons. (Apart from its pungent odour, the water from this well was intensely sulphurous, and when drunk, acted as a powerful laxative!)

In 1875, 'chemical analysis of the sulphur waters' was performed by Thomas E. Thorpe, Professor of Chemistry. It was demonstrated that over a dozen elements were present in the water which was:

proven to be highly beneficial in most forms of indigestion, constipation, flatulence, and acidity. For all cases of functional disorders of the liver. For stimulating the action of the kidneys and all forms of chronic skin diseases. To be drunk warm or cold. Dosage between 10–24 ounces to be taken early in the morning. It is further recorded that 'in one never to be forgotten morning in 1926, 1500 glasses of mineral water were served in the Royal Pump Room. Could one of these glasses have been drunk by Agatha herself?[1]

In 1878 the Old Swan Hotel was sold to the Harrogate Hydropathic Company, who redeveloped the site by building a replica of Doctor John Smedley's hydropathic establishment in Matlock,

Derbyshire. The Harrogate Hydropathic (The Hydro) had 200 bedrooms, a dining room for 300 'patients', coal fires in every bedroom and hot and cold running water. It was believed to be the first building in Harrogate to be lit by electricity.

In 1897 the Royal Baths, opened by HRH the Duke of Clarence, was one of the most advanced centres for hydrotherapy in the world. The medical baths employed bath attendants and masseurs, and facilities offered included Turkish baths, rest cubicles, vichy douches and electric shock baths.[2]

Appendix 5
The Lights on Agatha's Car

There are several factors that enter the equation to calculate the number of hours it took to discharge the battery on Agatha Christie's car. The unknown variables relate to the state of charge of the battery at the time of her accident: a) Was the car originally started using the electric starter, thus draining the battery, or was it hand cranked? b) Did Agatha select the 'charge' position on the dashboard switch during the journey to compensate for the load of the lighting? (There was no automatic charging regulator fitted to the Morris Cowley and, in fact, there was no indication to the driver when the battery was fully charged.) c) Did Agatha try to restart the car after the accident?

Finally, the ambient temperature affects the capacity of a battery and we know that the minimum temperature at the time was one degree Centigrade.

If we assume each headlight bulb was 36 watts (72 watts in total) and each sidelight was 6 watts (18 watts in total—there being just one rear light on the offside which also illuminated the number plate) then the total electrical load would have been 90 watts requiring a current of $90/12 = 7.5$ amps.

The battery, specified for the Cowley of the period, had a stated capacity of 56 amp-hr. The theoretical maximum number of hours before the battery was discharged would therefore be $56/7.5 = 7.5$ hours. However, in practice, it would have been significantly less than this figure, partly for the reasons given above but also because the specified capacity of 56 amp-hr was for a 20 hour discharge rate rather than the more rapid rate of 7.5 hours. Also, then as now, manufacturer's specifications were notoriously optimistic.[1]

Endnotes

Foreword
1. Cade, Jared, *Agatha Christie and the Eleven Missing Days*, pp. 131-2.
2. *Ibid..*, p. 312.
3. *Ibid..*, p. 132.

Chapter 1
1. Details obtained from a poster, issued by the Berkshire Constabulary, 9 December 1926. Courtesy Berkshire Record Office.
2. *Surrey Advertiser*, 11 December 1926.
3. Christie, Agatha, *An Autobiography, p.131.*
4. *The Times*, Tuesday 7 December 1926. It was not until the 1930s that this model of car was given the nickname 'Bullnose Morris Cowley'.
5. Railway Timetable, Summary Tables, kindly provided by the National Railway Museum, York.
6. Cade, Jared, *Agatha Christie and the Eleven Missing Days*, p. 83.
7. Morgan, Janet, *Agatha Christie: A Biography*, p. 155.
8. *Surrey Advertiser*, 11 December 1926.
9. *The Times, Wednesday 8 December 1926.*
10. Deputy Chief Constable William Kenward to A. L. Dixon, Home Office, Whitehall, 9 February 1927. Earlier that year, one of the firm's vehicles, an 'AC Six', had become the first British car to win the Monte Carlo Rally.
11. Surrey Advertiser, 11 December 1926.
12. Thompson, Laura, Agatha Christie: An English Mystery, jacket,
13. *Ibid..*, p. 225.
14. *Surrey Advertiser*, 11 December 1926.
15. *The Times*, Wednesday 8 December 1926.
16. The chalk pit has since been filled in and is now surrounded by trees.
17. Bourdon, M. W., *Motor Driving Made Easy: A Complete Guide for the Beginner, p. 121.*
18. *Met Office.*
19. *Surrey Advertiser*, 11 December 1926.
20. *The Times*, Tuesday 7 December 1926.
21. *Surrey Advertiser*, 11 December 1926.
22. Deputy Chief Constable William Kenward to A. L. Dixon, Home Office, Whitehall, 9 February 1927.
23. This is not to be confused with the Borough Police Station in North Street.
24. Morgan, Janet, *op. cit.*, p. 135.
25. Robyns, Gwen, *The Mystery of Agatha Christie, p. 61.*
26. Thompson, Laura, *op. cit.*, p. 177.
27. *The Daily Mail*, 15 December 1926.
28. *The Daily Mail*, 10 December 1926.
29. Robyns, Gwen, *op. cit.*, p. 62.
30. Morgan, Janet, *op. cit.*, p. 155.

31. *Ibid..*, p. 155.
32. Janet Morgan to the author, email, 10 March 2013.
33. Christie, Agatha, *op. cit.*, p.343.
34. Robyns, Gwen, *op. cit.*, p. 62.
35. Morgan, Janet, *op. cit.*, p. 156.
36. Thompson, Laura, *op. cit.*, p. 232.
37. Morgan, Janet, *op. cit.*, p. 155.
38. Cade, Jared, *op. cit.*, p. 90.
39. *Surrey Advertiser*, 11 December 1926.

Chapter 2
1. See Appendix 1.
2. Roberts, Tom, *Friends and Villains*, p. 58.
3. *The Times, Tuesday 7 December 1926.*
4. Cade, Jared, Agatha Christie and the Eleven Missing Days, p. 90.
5. *The Times*, Wednesday 8 December 1926.
6. *Surrey Advertiser*, 11 December 1926.
7. *Surrey Advertiser, 11 December 1926.*
8. Robyns, Gwen, The Mystery of Agatha Christie, p. 67.
9. The Times, Wednesday 8 December 1926.
10. Morgan, Janet, Agatha Christie: A Biography, p. 141.
11. *The Times*, Thursday 9 December 1926.
12. Morgan, Janet, *op. cit.*, p. 141.
13. British Postal Museum & Archive.
14. *The Times*, Wednesday 8 December 1926.
15. *The Times*, Thursday 9 December 1926.
16. *The Daily Mail, 10 December 1926.*
17. Gwen Robyns's biographies also include those of Vivien Leigh and Grace Kelly.
18. Robyns, Gwen, op. cit., pp. 67-8.
19. International Centre for the History of Crime, Policing and Justice, Part 2: Policing Wars and Consequences, 1902–1950.
20. *The Daily Mail*, 10 December 1926.
21. *The Daily Mail*, 10 December 1926.
22. *The Daily Mail, 10 December 1926.*
23. Deputy Chief Constable William Kenward to A. L. Dixon, Home Office, Whitehall, 9 February 1927.
24. 22 February 1927, Commissioner of Police of the Metropolis to Secretary of State, The National Archives, HO45/25904.
25. Deputy Chief Constable William Kenward to A. L. Dixon, Home Office, Whitehall, 9 February 1927.
26. The National Archives, HO45/25904.
27. The National Archives, HO45/25904.
28. The National Archives, HO45/25904.
29. Deputy Chief Constable William Kenward to A. L. Dixon, Home Office, Whitehall, 9 February 1927.
30. The National Archives, HO45/25904.

Chapter 3
1. *The Daily Mail*, 10 December 1926.
2. *The Daily Mail*, 10 December 1926.
3. *The Daily Mail*, 10 December 1926.
4. *The Daily Mail*, 10 December 1926.
5. *The Daily Mail, 10 December 1926.*
6. Robyns, Gwen, The Mystery of Agatha Christie, p. 61.
7. *The Daily Mail*, 10 December 1926.
8. *The Daily Mail*, 10 December 1926.

 9. *The Daily Mail*, 10 December 1926.
10. *The Daily Mail*, 10 December 1926.
11. *The Daily Mail*, 10 December 1926.
12. *The Daily Mail*, 10 December 1926.
13. *Surrey Advertiser*, 11 December 1926.
14. Thompson, Laura, *Agatha Christie: An English Mystery*, p. 233.
15. *The Daily Mail*, 10 December 1926.
16. Roberts, Tom, *Friends and Villains*, p. 18.
17. *Ibid.*, p. 33.
18. *Ibid.*, p. 33.
19. *Ibid., pp. 33-4. Appendix 2.*
20. Morgan, Janet, Agatha Christie: A Biography, p. 149.

Chapter 4

 1. *Indge, Sergeant W., A Short History of the Berkshire Constabulary*, p. 125. Appendix 3.
 2. Morgan, Janet, *Agatha Christie: A Biography*, p. 146.
 3. Robyns, Gwen, *The Mystery of Agatha Christie, p. 70.*
 4. Ibid., p. 70.
 5. Cade, Jared, Agatha Christie and the Eleven Missing Days, pp. 141-2.
 6. *Morgan, Janet, op. cit.*, p. 146.
 7. *The Times*, 13 December 1926.
 8. *The Times*, 14 December 1926.
 9. *The Times, 14 December 1926.*

Chapter 5

 1. *The Daily Mail*, 15 December 1926.
 2. *The Daily Mail*, 15 December 1926.
 3. *Harrogate Advertiser*, 18 December 1926.
 4. *The Daily Mail*, 15 December 1926.
 5. *The Daily Mail*, 15 December 1926.
 6. *The Daily Mail, 15 December 1926.*
 7. Robyns, Gwen, The Mystery of Agatha Christie, p. 74.
 8. *The Daily Mail*, 15 December 1926.
 9. *Harrogate Advertiser*, 18 December 1926.
10. *Harrogate Advertiser*, 18 December 1926.
11. *The Times*, 16 December 1926.
12. *Harrogate Advertiser*, 18 December 1926.
13. *The Daily Mail*, 15 December 1926.
14. Robyns, Gwen, *op. cit.*, p. 72.
15. *Harrogate Advertiser*, 18 December 1926.
16. *Harrogate Advertiser, 18 December 1926.*
17. The second number on the newspaper report is illegible, but is probably either a '1', giving the time of 11 p.m., or possibly a '2', giving a time of midnight.
18. *Harrogate Advertiser*, 18 December 1926.
19. *Harrogate Advertiser*, 18 December 1926.
20. Robyns, Gwen, *op. cit.*, p. 70.
21. *Ibid., pp. 70-1.*
22. Railway Timetable, Summary Tables, kindly provided by the National Railway Museum, York.
23. *The Daily Mail*, 15 December 1926.
24. *The Daily Mail*, 15 December 1926.
25. *The Daily Mail, 15 December 1926.*
26. 'Nulon'—An unidentified material. There was no nylon at that time.
27. *The Daily Mail*, 15 December 1926.

28. Thompson, Laura, *Agatha Christie: An English Mystery*, p. 243.
29. Robyns, Gwen, *op. cit.*, p. 81.
30. Thompson, Laura, *op. cit.*, p. 194.
31. Morgan, Janet, *Agatha Christie: A Biography, p. 149.*
32. *Thompson, Laura, op. cit.*, p. 204.
33. *Ibid., p. 218.*

Chapter 6
1. The Daily Mail, 15 December 1926.
2. Robyns, Gwen, The Mystery of Agatha Christie, p. 76.
3. *The Times*, 16 December 1926.
4. Christie, Agatha, *An Autobiography*, p. 365.
5. *The Times*, 16 December 1926.
6. *Harrogate Advertiser, 18 December 1926.*
7. Diagnostic and Statistical Manual of Mental Disorders, 4th Edition, American Psychiatric Association, p. 172.
8. *The Daily Mail*, 15 December 1926.
9. Robyns, Gwen, *op. cit.*, pp. 62-3.
10. *Ibid.*, p. 63.
11. *The Times, 17 December 1926.*
12. *Donald Elms Core, 1882–1934.*
13. Cade, Jared, Agatha Christie and the Eleven Missing Days, p. 152.
14. Ibid., p. 156.
15. Rosalind Hicks, Obituary, The Telegraph (online), November 2004.
16. Thompson, Laura, *Agatha Christie: An English Mystery*, p. 251.
17. The cigarette case was sold at auction at Sotheby's, London, on 10 July 2012.
18. Robyns, Gwen, *op. cit.*, p. 88.
19. *The Times*, 21 April 1928.

Chapter 7
1. *The Daily Mail*, 16 February 1926.
2. Oxford Dictionaries (online).
3. *The Daily Mail*, 16 February 1926.
4. Thompson, Laura, *Agatha Christie: An English Mystery*, pp. 189-90.

Chapter 8
1. Robyns, Gwen, *The Mystery of Agatha Christie*, p. 64. See Calder, Lord Ritchie, *New Statesmen, January 1976.*
2. Ibid., p. 64
3. British Postal Museum & Archive.
4. *Kelly's Directory*, 1926, Reading Local Studies Library.
5. Robyns, Gwen, *op. cit.*, pp. 84-5. Jared Cade asserts that no evidence has been found to confirm that Gladys was employed in an official capacity by the Berkshire Constabulary. Cade, Jared, *Agatha Christie and the Eleven Missing Days, p. 285. However, the title 'Confidential Secretary' may simply have meant that she attended to her father's paperwork and perhaps did some typing for him, on an unofficial basis.*
6. *Robyns, Gwen, op. cit.*, p. 85.
7. *Ibid.*, p. 72
8. *Ibid., p. 85.*
9. *National Archives, HO45/25904.*
10. *National Archives, HO 45/25904.*
11. Deputy Chief Constable William Kenward to A. L. Dixon, Home Office, Whitehall, 9 February 1927.

Chapter 9

1. *Morgan, Janet, Agatha Christie: A Biography*, p. 155.
2. Cade, Jared, *Agatha Christie and the Eleven Missing Days*, p. 75.
3. Robyns, Gwen, *The Mystery of Agatha Christie*, p. 72.
4. *Ibid.*, p. 85.
5. *The Times*, Wednesday 8 December 1926.
6. Morgan, Janet, *op. cit.*, p. 141.
7. *The Times*, Thursday 9 December 1926.
8. Thompson, Laura, *Agatha Christie: An English Mystery*, p. 194.
9. *The Times*, Wednesday 8 December 1926.
10. Christie, Agatha, *An Autobiography*, p. 365.
11. Thompson, Laura, *op. cit.*, p. 202.
12. *Ibid., p. 197.*

Chapter 10

1. *Christie, Agatha, An Autobiography*, p. 17.
2. *Ibid.*, p. 17.
3. *Ibid.*, p. 19.
4. *Ibid.*, p. 13.
5. *Ibid.*, p. 19.
6. *Ibid.*, pp. 13-14.
7. *Ibid.*, pp. 56, 47.
8. *Ibid.*, p. 66.
9. *Ibid.*, p. 82.
10. *Ibid.*, p. 95.
11. *Ibid.*, p. 24.
12. *Ibid.*, p. 112.
13. *Ibid.*, p. 35.
14. *Ibid.*, p. 120.
15. *Ibid.*, p. 137.
16. *Ibid.*, pp. 110-111.
17. *Ibid.*, p. 60.
18. *Ibid.*, p. 47.
19. *Ibid.*, p. 59.
20. *Ibid.*, p. 108.
21. *Ibid.*, p. 85.
22. *Ibid.*, p. 109.
23. *Ibid.*, pp. 20-22.
24. *Ibid.*, pp. 32-3.
25. *Ibid.*, p. 58.
26. *Ibid.*, p. 60.
27. *Ibid.*, pp. 58-9.
28. *Ibid.*, pp. 99-101.
29. *Ibid.*, pp. 123-4.
30. *Ibid.*, pp. 156-9.
31. *Ibid.*, p. 203.
32. *Ibid.*, pp. 165, 188-9.
33. *Ibid.*, p. 195.
34. *Ibid.*, pp. 130-1.
35. *Ibid.*, pp. 172, 175, 177.
36. *Ibid.*, pp. 200-01.
37. *Ibid.*, p. 217.

Chapter 11

1. Christie, Agatha, *An Autobiography*, p. 211.
2. *Ibid.*, pp. 134-5.
3. *Ibid.*, p. 64.
4. *Ibid.*, p. 220.
5. *Ibid.*, p. 227.
6. *Ibid.*, p. 364.
7. *Ibid.*, pp. 332-3.
8. *Ibid.*, p. 332.
9. *Ibid.*, p. 83.
10. *The Times*, 21 April 1928.
11. Christie, Agatha, *op. cit.*, p. 254.
12. *Ibid.*, pp. 257-8.
13. *Ibid.*, p. 261.
14. *Ibid.*, p. 263.
15. *Ibid., p. 284.*
16. Thompson, Laura, Agatha Christie: An English Mystery, p. 101.

Chapter 12

1. Christie, Agatha, *An Autobiography*, p. 36.
2. *Ibid.*, p. 36.
3. *Diagnostic and Statistical Manual of Mental Disorders*, Fourth Edition, American Psychiatric Association, pp. 631, 633.
4. *Ibid., pp. 634-6.*
5. *Hoover,* John H. *John Bowlby on Human Attachment, http://www.cyc-net.org/cyc.online/cycol-0304-bowlby.html 18.01.2006.*
6. *Hoover, John H., op. cit.*
7. Christie, Agatha, *op. cit.*, p. 153.
8. *Ibid.*, p. 104.
9. *Ibid.*, p. 105.
10. *Ibid.*, p. 116.
11. *Ibid.*, p. 24.
12. Westmacott, Mary, *Unfinished Portrait*, p. 28.
13. Christie, Agatha, *op. cit.*, p. 35.
14. Westmacott, Mary, *op. cit.*, p. 116.
15. Hall, Calvin S., *The Meaning of Dreams, p. 53.*

Chapter 13

1. *Christie, Agatha, An Autobiography*, p. 341.
2. *Ibid.*, p. 346.
3. *Ibid.*, p. 345.
4. *Ibid.*, pp. 349-50.
5. *Ibid.*, p. 350.
6. *Ibid.*, p. 353.
7. *Ibid.*, p. 357.
8. *Ibid.*, p. 359.
9. *Ibid.*, p. 358.
10. *Ibid.*, p. 359.
11. *Ibid.*, p. 361.
12. *Ibid.*, p. 362.
13. *Ibid.*, p. 363.
14. *Ibid.*, p. 363-4.
15. *Daily Express*, 24 January 1927.

16. Christie, Agatha, *op. cit., p. 364.*
17. *Cade, Jared, Agatha Christie and the Eleven Missing Days,* p. 162.
18. Christie, Agatha, *op. cit.,* p. 371.

Chapter 14
1. Westmacott, Mary, *Unfinished Portrait,* p. 11.
2. *Ibid.,* p. 9.
3. *Ibid.,* p. 10.
4. *Ibid.,* p. 11.
5. *Ibid.,* p. 11.
6. *Ibid.,* p. 9.
7. *Ibid.,* p. 24.
8. *Ibid.,* p. 24.
9. *Ibid.,* p. 48.
10. *Ibid.,* p. 127.
11. *Ibid.,* p. 104.
12. *Ibid.,* p. 129.
13. *Ibid.,* p. 130.
14. *Ibid.,* p. 60.
15. *Ibid.,* p. 124.
16. *Ibid.,* pp. 145-6.
17. *Ibid.,* p. 189.
18. *Ibid.,* p. 119.
19. *Ibid.,* p. 78.
20. *Ibid.,* pp. 115-6.
21. *Ibid.,* p. 213.
22. *Ibid.,* p. 214.
23. *Ibid.,* p. 216.
24. *Ibid.,* p. 218.
25. *Ibid.,* p. 219.
26. *Ibid.,* p. 235.
27. *Ibid.,* p. 232.
28. *Ibid.,* p. 221.
29. *Ibid.,* p. 224.
30. *Ibid.,* p. 226.
31. *Ibid.,* p. 233.
32. *Ibid.,* p. 234.
33. Christie, Agatha, *An Autobiography,* p. 395.
34. Westmacott, Mary, *op. cit.,* p .236.
35. *Ibid.,* p. 241.
36. *Ibid.,* p. 245.
37. *Ibid.,* p. 245.
38. *Ibid.,* p. 284.
39. *Ibid.,* p. 290.
40. *Ibid.,* p. 253.
41. *Ibid.,* p. 282.
42. *Ibid.,* p. 291.
43. *Ibid.,* p. 291-3.
44. *Ibid.,* p. 307.
45. *Ibid.,* p. 298-9.
46. *Ibid.,* pp. 299-300.
47. *Ibid.,* pp. 301-2.
48. *Ibid.,* p. 315.

49. *Ibid.*, p. 315.
50. *Ibid.*, p. 327.
51. *Ibid.*, pp. 332-3.
52. *Ibid.*, p. 333.
53. *Ibid.*, p. 339.
54. *Ibid.*, p. 344.
55. *Ibid.*, pp. 346-7.
56. *Ibid.*, p. 349.
57. *Ibid.*, p. 350.
58. *Ibid.*, pp. 352, 354.
59. *Ibid.*, p. 356.
60. Christie, Agatha, *op. cit.*, pp. 360, 362.
61. Westmacott, Mary, *op. cit.*, p. 357.
62. *Ibid.*, p. 358.
63. *Ibid.*, p. 361.
64. *Ibid.*, p. 362.
65. *Ibid.*, pp. 363-5.
66. *Diagnostic and Statistical Manual of Mental Disorders*, fourth Edition, American Psychiatric Association, p. 690.
67. Westmacott, Mary, *op. cit.*, pp. 363-5.
68. *Ibid.*, pp. 366-7.
69. *Ibid.*, p. 367.
70. *Ibid.*, pp. 368-9.
71. *Ibid.*, p. 370.
72. *Ibid.*, pp. 370-1.
73. *Ibid.*, pp. 371-2.
74. *Ibid.*, p. 372.
75. *Ibid.*, p. 373.
76. *Ibid.*, p. 373.
77. *Ibid.*, p. 374.
78. *Ibid.*, p. 379.
79. *Ibid.*, pp. 381-2.
80. *Ibid.*, p. 384.
81. *Ibid.*, p. 17.
82. *Ibid.*, p. 400.
83. Westmacott, Mary, *op. cit.*, jacket cover.
84. Christie, Agatha, *op. cit.*, p. 487.

Chapter 15
1. Christie, Agatha, *An Autobiography*, p. 364.
2. *Ibid.*, p. 369.
3. *The Medical Directory* (Provinces), 1927.
4. Published in *Journal of Tuberculosis*, and probably relating to the efficacy of that region's particular climate in restoring the health of the tuberculosis suffers in the sanatorium at Banchory, where he had worked.
5. Both papers were published in the *British Medical Journal*.
6. *Christie, Agatha, op. cit.*, pp. 369-70.

Chapter 16
1. Cade, Jared, *Agatha Christie and the Eleven Missing Days*, p. 15.
2. Thompson, Laura, *Agatha Christie: An English Mystery*, p. 247.
3. Cade, Jared, *op. cit.*, p. 298.
4. *Ibid.*, p. 15.
5. *Ibid.*, p. 129.

6. *Ibid.*, p. 245.
7. *Ibid.*, p. 75.
8. *Ibid.*, p. 131.
9. *Ibid., pp. 131-2.*
10. Robyns, Gwen, The Mystery of Agatha Christie, p. 62.
11. *The Daily Mail*, 16 February 1926.
12. Cade, Jared, *op. cit.*, pp. 131-2.
13. *Ibid.*, p. 107.
14. Christie, Agatha, *An Autobiography*, pp. 119-203.
15. Agatha mistakenly stated that the marriage took place during the First World War.
16. Christie, Agatha, *op. cit.*, p. 270.
17. *Ibid.*, p. 347.
18. Cade, Jared, *op. cit.*, p. 132.
19. *Ibid.*, p. 131.
20. *Ibid.*, p. 132.
21. *The Times*, Wednesday 8 December 1926.
22. Cade, Jared, *op. cit.*, p. 306.
23. *Ibid., pp. 305-6.*
24. *Ibid., pp. 132-3.*
25. Thompson, Laura, *op. cit.*, p. 194.
26. Cade, Jared, *op. cit.*, p. 133.
27. *Ibid., pp. 133-4*
28. *Ibid.*, p. 119. The telephone number for Styles was 'Ascot 375'. Heritage Team, Maidenhead Library, Maidenhead, Berkshire.
29. Robyns, Gwen, *op. cit.*, p. 76.
30. Cade, Jared, *op. cit.*, p. 196.

Chapter 17
1. *The Daily Mail*, 16 February 1926.
2. Morgan, Janet, *Agatha Christie: A Biography*, p. 154.
3. Robyns, Gwen, *The Mystery of Agatha Christie*, p. 64.
4. Deputy Chief Constable William Kenward to A. L. Dixon, Home Office, Whitehall, 9 February 1927.
5. Deputy Chief Constable William Kenward to A. L. Dixon, Home Office, Whitehall, 9 February 1927.
6. Calculated for the Kew station, situated 16 miles to the north of Newlands Corner. Information kindly supplied by the Met. Office National Meteorological Archive.
7. Bourdon, M. W., *Motor Driving Made Easy: A Complete Guide for the Beginner*, p. 118.
8. *Ibid.*, pp. 119-20.
9. *Ibid.*, pp. 174-5.
10. Information kindly supplied by Malcolm McKay.
11. Bourdon, M. W., *op. cit.*, p. 11.
12. Thompson, Laura, *Agatha Christie: An English Mystery*, pp. 252-3.
13. *The Daily Mail*, 16 February 1926.
14. Thompson, Laura, *op. cit.*, p. 193.
15. *The Times*, Wednesday 8 December 1926.
16. Oxford Dictionaries (online).
17. *Diagnostic and Statistical Manual of Mental Disorders*, fourth Edition, American Psychiatric Association, pp. 760-1.

Chapter 18
1. Railway Timetable, Summary Tables, kindly provided by the National Railway Museum, York.
2. *Harrogate Advertiser, 18 December 1926.*
3. Morgan, Janet, *Agatha Christie: A Biography*, p. 149.
4. Information kindly supplied by the National Railway Museum, York.

Chapter 19
1. Christie, Agatha, *The Secret Adversary* p. 109.
2. *Ibid.*, pp. 109-110.
3. *Ibid.*, p. 110.
4. *Ibid.*, p. 154.
5. *Ibid.*, pp. 197-8.
6. *Ibid.*, p. 201.
7. *Ibid., p. 201.*
8. Christie, Agatha, Hercule Poirot: the Complete Short Stories, p. 41.
9. *Ibid.*, p. 42.
10. *Ibid.*, p. 42.
11. *Ibid.*, p. 42.
12. Christie, Agatha, *The Edge*, p. 9.
13. *Ibid.*, p. 24.
14. Westmacott, Mary, *Giant's Bread,* p. 474.
15. *Ibid.*, p. 454.
16. *Ibid.*, p. 467.
17. Christie, Agatha, *Harlequin's Lane*, pp. 364-5.
18. *Ibid.*, p. 384.
19. *Ibid.*, p. 389.
20. *Ibid.*, p. 394.
21. *Ibid.*, pp. 395-6.

Chapter 20
1. Robyns, Gwen, *The Mystery of Agatha Christie*, pp. 81-2.
2. *Ibid.*, p. 82.
3. *Ibid.*, p. 83.
4. *Ibid., p. 83.*
5. *Ludwig, A. M. (1983), 'The Psychobiological Functions of Dissociation'. American Journal of Clinical Hypnosis*, 26: p. 93.
6. American Psychiatric Association, 1994, Coons, Philip M. 'Psychogenic or Dissociative Fugue: A Clinical Investigation of Five Cases'.
7. *Ibid.*
8. *Diagnostic and Statistical Manual of Mental Disorders*, fourth Edition, American Psychiatric Association, p. 525.
9. Oxford Dictionaries (online).
10. *Diagnostic and Statistical Manual of Mental Disorders, op. cit.*, p. 524.
11. Van der Hart, Onno, and Rutner Horst, 'The Dissociation Theory of Pierre Janet', Journal of Traumatic Stress, Volume 2, Number 4, 1989.
12. Hacking, Ian, *Mad Travellers: Reflections on the Reality of Transient Mental Illness*, pp. 1, 7, 13-14, 19.
13. *Ibid.*, pp. 13, 14.
14. *Ibid.*, p. 8.
15. 'Ueber Fugues und Fugue—ähnliche Zustände', Jahrb. F. Psychiat. 23:107, 1903.
16. Ziegler, Lloyd H., 'Hysterical Fugues', Journal of the American Medical Association, Volume 101, Number 8, pp. 571-6.
17. Rosalind Hicks, Obituary, *The Telegraph* (online), 13 November 2004.
18. Coons, Philip M. 'Psychogenic or Dissociative Fugue: A Clinical Investigation of Five Cases'.

Chapter 21
1. Morgan, Janet, *Agatha Christie: A Biography*, p. 159.
2. Janet Morgan, email to Dr Andrew Norman, 10 November 2012.
3. Sophia Schutts, email to Dr Andrew Norman, 29 October 2012.
4. Morgan, Janet, *op. cit., p. 159.*

Chapter 22

1. Morgan, Janet, *Agatha Christie: A Biography*, p. 134.
2. Railway Timetable, Summary Tables, kindly provided by the National Railway Museum, York.
3. Congreve, William (1670-1729) *The Old Bachelor*. III. viii.
4. *The Daily Mail, 16 February 1926*.
5. American Psychiatric Association, 1994, Coons, Philip M. 'Psychogenic or Dissociative Fugue: A Clinical Investigation of Five Cases'.
6. Railway Timetable, Summary Tables, kindly provided by the National Railway Museum, York.
7. Thompson, Laura, *Agatha Christie: An English Mystery*, p. 194.
8. Robyns, Gwen, *The Mystery of Agatha Christie, p. 83.*
9. Thompson, Laura, *op. cit.*, p. 252.
10. *Ibid., p. 251.*
11. Cade, Jared, Agatha Christie and the Eleven Missing Days, p. 168.
12. *Ibid.*, p. 168.
13. *Ibid.*, p. 172.
14. *Ibid.*, p. 172.
15. Morgan, Janet, *op. cit.*, p. 134.
16. *The Times*, 16 February 1928.
17. Christie, Agatha, *Why Didn't They Ask Evans*, p. 81.
18. *Ibid.*, pp. 143, 145.
19. *Ibid.*, p. 168.
20. *Ibid.*, p. 210.
21. *Ibid.*, p. 230.

Chapter 23

1. Christie, Agatha, *An Autobiography*, p. 372.
2. *Ibid.*, pp. 387-8.
3. *Ibid.*, p. 404.
4. *Ibid.*, p. 414.
5. *Ibid.*, p. 417.
6. *Ibid.*, p. 409.
7. *Ibid.*, p. 429.
8. *Ibid.*, p. 430.
9. *Ibid.*, p. 395.
10. *Ibid.*, p. 449. Miss Marple had already appeared in a short story entitled *The Tuesday Night Club* (1927).
11. *Ibid.*, p. 483.
12. *Ibid., p. 479.*
13. Morgan, Janet, *Agatha Christie: A Biography*, p. 205.
14. Matthew, H. C. G. and Brian Harrison (editors), *Oxford Dictionary of National Biography*, Volume 36, p. 347.
15. Christie, Agatha, *op. cit.*, p. 521.
16. *Ibid.*, p. 542.
17. *Ibid.*, p. 546.
18. *Ibid.*, pp. 547-8.
19. Christie, Agatha, *Murder in Mesopotamia*, p. 162.
20. *Ibid.*, p. 40.
21. Christie, Agatha, *op. cit.*, pp. 532-3.
22. *Ibid., p. 535.*
23. In 2000, the family donated 'Greenway', together with its garden and Lower Greenway Farm, to the National Trust, and in 2006, a £5.4 million restoration of the house began.
24. Robyns, Gwen, *The Mystery of Agatha Christie*, pp. 213-6.

Chapter 24
1. *Amos* 5:24.
2. Christie, Agatha, *An Autobiography*, p. 24.
3. *Ibid.*, p. 39.
4. *Ibid.*, p. 49.
5. *Ibid.*, p. 80.
6. *Ibid.*, p. 109.
7. *Ibid.*, p. 197.
8. *Ibid.*, p. 128.
9. *Ibid.*, p. 216.
10. *Ibid.*, p. 260.
11. Christie, Agatha, *Five Little Pigs, p. 18.*

Epilogue
1. *Christie, Agatha, An Autobiography, p. 118.*
2. *Ibid.*, p. 550.
3. *Ibid.*, p. 116.
4. *Ibid.*, p. 113.
5. *Ibid.*, p. 120.
6. *Ibid.*, p. 47.
7. Gray, Thomas, *Elegy in a Country Churchyard.*
8. Christie, Agatha, *op. cit.*, p. 25.
9. *Ibid.*, p. 317.
10. Thompson, Laura, *Agatha Christie: An English Mystery*, p. 484.

Appendix 1
1. Surrey Constabulary: *Appointment Book.*
2. Bartlett, Robert and The Open University, International Centre for the History of Crime Policing and Justice, Part 2: Policing Wars and Consequences 1902-1950, 2013.
3. *Ibid.*
4. Roberts, Tom, *Friends and Villains*, p. 56.
5. *Ibid.*, p. 58.
6. *Ibid.*, p. 55.
7. Bartlett, Robert, *op. cit.*
8. Roberts, Tom, *op. cit.*, p. 54.

Appendix 3
1. Indge, Sergeant W., A Short History of the Berkshire Constabulary, p. 125.
2. *Ibid.*, p. 82.
3. *Ibid., p. 51.*

Appendix 4
1. 'The Sulphur Waters: Stinking Well, Chemical Analysis by Thorpe in 1875'.
2. Information kindly supplied by The Old Swan Hotel, Harrogate.

Appendix 5
1. Information kindly supplied by Malcolm McKay of The Bullnose Morris Club.

Acknowledgments

Chris Atkins, Janet Morgan, Robert Bartlett, Mark Beswick, Natalie Burton, Alison Day, Patrick Collins, Vic Davis, Zizi Easun, Ceryl Evans, David Ford, Malcolm Holt, Stephen Laing, Anne Martin, John McGoldrick, Malcolm McKay, Penny McMahon; Edward Mortimer, Barbara Peirce, Den Petchey, Colin Probin, Chris Roberts, Sophia Schutts, Michael Sharpe, Ann Smith, Diana and Alan Turner, Laura Walker, Ros Watson, Cornelis de Wet; Stuart Wetherell,

Berkshire Record Office, Reading, Berkshire; British Motor Industry Heritage Trust; British Postal Museum & Archive; Bullnose Morris Club; Harrogate Library & Customer Services Centre, Harrogate, North Yorkshire; British Motor Industry Heritage Centre, Gaydon, Warwickshire; Mercer Gallery, Swan Road, Harrogate; Met. Office National Meteorological Archive, Sowton, Exeter; National Railway Museum, York; Poole Hospital Library; Reading Borough Libraries; Royal Borough of Windsor and Maidenhead, Local Information & Studies; Surrey History Centre, Woking; The Telephone Museum, Milton Keynes, Buckinghamshire.

I am deeply grateful to my beloved wife Rachel for all her help and encouragement.

About the Author

Andrew Norman was born in Newbury, Berkshire, UK in 1943. Having been educated at Thornhill High School, Gwelo, Southern Rhodesia (now Zimbabwe) and St Edmund Hall, Oxford, he qualified in medicine at the Radcliffe Infirmary. He has two children, Bridget and Thomas, by his first wife.

From 1972–83, Andrew worked as a general practitioner in Poole, Dorset, before a spinal injury cut short his medical career. He is now an established writer whose published works include biographies of Thomas Hardy, T. E. Lawrence, Sir Francis Drake, Adolf Hitler, Enid Blyton, Charles Darwin, and Beatrix Potter. Andrew was remarried to Rachel in 2005.

Bibliography

Autocar Handbook, The: A Guide to the Motor Car, Eleventh Edition (Iliffe, London, c. 1923)

Bourdon, M. W. *Motor Driving Made Easy: A Complete Guide for the Beginner*, Fourth Edition (Iliffe, London, c. 1925)

Cade, Jared, *Agatha Christie and the Eleven Missing Days* (Peter Owen, London, 2011)

Christie, Agatha, *An Autobiography* (HarperCollins, London, 1993)

Christie, Agatha, *Five Little Pigs* (Harper, London, 2007)

Christie, Agatha, *Hercule Poirot: the Complete Short Stories (HarperCollinsPublishers, London, 1999)*

Christie, Agatha, Murder in Mesopotamia (HarperCollins, London, 2008)

Christie, Agatha, *The Edge*, in *The Harlequin Tea Set* (G.P. Putnam, New York, 1997)

Christie, Agatha, *The Secret Adversary* (Triad/Granada, London, 1976)

Christie, Agatha, *Why Didn't They Ask Evans* (Heron Books, London, 1934)

Coons, Philip M. 'Psychogenic or Dissociative Fugue: A Clinical Investigation of Five Cases', Psychological Reports 1999, 84, 881, 886.

Diagnostic and Statistical Manual of Mental Disorders, fourth edition (American Psychiatric Association, 2007)

Gregory, Richard L. (editor), *The Oxford Companion to the Mind* (Oxford University Press, 1987)

Hacking, Ian, *Mad Travellers: Reflections on the Reality of Transient Mental Illness* (Harvard University Press, 1998)

Hall, Calvin S., *The Meaning of Dreams* (Harper, New York, 1953)

Indge, Sergeant W., *A Short History of the Berkshire Constabulary 1856–1956* (Baylis & Company, Maidenhead, 1956)

Matthew, H. C. G. and Brian Harrison (editors), *Oxford Dictionary of National Biography* (Oxford University Press, 2004)

Morgan, Janet, *Agatha Christie: A Biography* (Fontana/Collins, Glasgow, 1985)

Norman, Andrew, *Agatha Christie: The Finished Portrait* (Tempus, Stroud, Gloucestershire, 2006)

Roberts, Tom, *Friends and Villains* (Ulverscroft, Leicester, 1987)

Robyns, Gwen, *The Mystery of Agatha Christie* (Chivers Press, Bath, 1990)

Surrey Constabulary: *Appointment Book*.

Smith, Dr Tony, *The British Medical Association: Complete Family Health Encyclopedia* (Dorling Kindersley, London, 1990)

Thompson, Laura. *Agatha Christie: An English Mystery* (Headline Review, London, 2007)

Westmacott, Mary, *Giant's Bread* (HarperCollins, London, 2009)

Westmacott, Mary, *Unfinished Portrait* (HarperCollins, London, 2009)

Index